THE FEDERAL CITY: PLANS & REALITIES

THE FEDERAL CITY: PLANS & REALITIES

THE HISTORY: Frederick Gutheim

THE EXHIBITION: Wilcomb E. Washburn

SMITHSONIAN INSTITUTION

NATIONAL CAPITAL PLANNING COMMISSION

COMMISSION OF FINE ARTS

Published in cooperation with the National Capital Planning Commission
by the Smithsonian Institution Press Washington DC 1976

Designed by Hubert Leckie

Smithsonian Institution Press publication number: 6161

Printed in the United States by Stephenson Inc.

Library of Congress Cataloging in Publication Data
Gutheim, Frederick Albert, 1908–
The Federal City.
Sponsored by the Smithsonian Institution, in cooperation with the National Capital Planning
Commission and the Commission of Fine Arts and held at the Smithsonian Institution.
Includes bibliographies and index.
Supt. of Docs. No.: SI 1.2:F31
1 Cities and towns—Planning—Washington, D.C.—Exhibitions.
2 Cities and towns—Planning—Washington, D.C.—History.
I. Washburn, Wilcomb E. II. Smithsonian Institution. III. Title
NA9127.W2G87   711'.4'097530740153   75-619412

CONTENTS

Illustrations

Acknowledgments

The Smithsonian Institution, the National Capital Planning Commission, and the Commission of Fine Arts are grateful to the following for materials used in the exhibition and this book: Library of Congress; National Archives; Columbia Historical Society; Pennsylvania Avenue Development Corporation; National Capital Parks, U.S. Department of Interior; U.S. Army Corps of Engineers; Martin Luther King Memorial Library (D.C. Public Library); Gallaudet College; American Antiquarian Society; Metropolitan Museum of Art; Boston Public Library; New York Public Library; Library Company of Philadelphia; Virginia Department of Highways; Professor Charles McLaughlin; Professor George B. Tatum; University of Rochester; *Washington Post*; *Washington Star*; International Museum of Photography at George Eastman House; National Geographic Society; Federal Aviation Agency, U.S. Department of Transportation; U.S. Army Air Corps; Chloethiel Woodard Smith; Washington Metropolitan Area Transit Authority; Fairchild Aerial Services, Inc.; George Washington University Wright Collection; The White House Collection; Historical American Buildings Survey; Turner Associates; National War College; Benjamin Lawless; Donald E. Jackson.

In addition, the following individuals provided assistance in organizing the exhibition: Staples & Charles, Washington, D.C., designers of the exhibition; James Goode; Marsha Mateyka; Cheryl Hayes; Perry Fisher and Robert Truax of the Columbia Historical Society; Ralph Ehrenberg of the Cartographic Reference Branch of the National Archives; Paul Spreiregen; Professor Chandler Screven of the University of Wisconsin; and Susan Daumit.

The book has been edited by Ruth Spiegel of the Smithsonian Institution Press.

Forewords

Smithsonian Institution

The Smithsonian Institution is proud to sponsor, in cooperation with the National Capital Planning Commission and the Commission of Fine Arts, the exhibition on *The Federal City: Plans and Realities*. The exhibition is about planning Washington, and in particular about planning the development of the monumental core as designed by Pierre L'Enfant. The Mall, where the Smithsonian is situated, constitutes the heart of the monumental core, and visitors to the Smithsonian, as they cross between museums, gaze on two of the principal foci planned by L'Enfant: the Capitol and the Washington Monument. Surely there can be no more majestic setting for events of a national character. Surely there can be no more symbolic ground for the heart of the nation!

Yet, in spite of its serene and stately appearance today, the Mall area and how it should be treated in function, in landscaping, and in building have been points of continued controversy and debate since the very beginning. L'Enfant's scheme, which saw a Grand Avenue four hundred feet down the Mall—reminiscent of the Champs Élysées in Paris—was not realized. Andrew Jackson Downing's more naturalistic proposal of 1851, with its plantings and curving carriage and walking paths, was similarly aborted and eventually discarded. Even the plan of the Senate Park Commission of 1901, which foresaw the elimination of the Smithsonian Building and a formalistic treatment of the space, was modified before being put into partial effect.

President George Washington had his heart set on a university in the new capital and Benjamin Latrobe designed a scheme for it (remarkably like that of Jefferson's University of Virginia) in the area of the Mall closest to the Washington Monument. Although a university in Washington's name eventually developed in the nation's capital, it did not develop as he foresaw it. Perhaps, on the Mall, the Smithsonian Institution inherited the mantle of academic excellence Washington sought for the monumental city.

The Smithsonian, under its first Secretary, Joseph Henry, played a key role in reactivating a comprehensive plan for the capital in the 1850s. It was Henry, and William Corcoran, the local financier, who convinced President Millard Fillmore to hire Downing to redeem Washington from physical neglect, as Henry had redeemed Washington from intellectual neglect.

The Federal City: Plans and Realities will continue in the Great Hall of James Renwick's Smithsonian Institution Building for two years. It is our hope that the exhibition will inspire Washington's residents and visitors to be concerned with Washington, as well as their own cities wherever they may be, and to prevent neglect from becoming the heritage of the twenty-first century.

S. Dillon Ripley, *Secretary*, SMITHSONIAN INSTITUTION

The Commission of Fine Arts

The creation of the Commission of Fine Arts had its origin in the growing sense of civic pride which reached its peak in the early years of this century. Specifically, the commission was the outgrowth of the events associated with the celebration of the capital's Centennial in 1900 and the plan for Washington developed in 1901 and published in 1902. Referred to usually as the McMillan or Senate Park Commission Plan, this set of proposals was based on the original plan for Washington by Pierre L'Enfant.

Created by act of Congress in 1910, the Commission of Fine Arts was, in its early years, especially conscious of its role in implementing the 1902 plan. A large part of what the visitor sees in Washington today—the present Mall, the Lincoln Memorial, and much of the park system—is the result of the work of the Commission of Fine Arts in this direction. In fact, two Senate Park Commission members, Daniel H. Burnham and Frederick Law Olmsted, Jr., were among the first appointees to the Commission of Fine Arts.

Throughout its existence, the Commission of Fine Arts has continued to be concerned with long-range plans for the City of Washington. It shares this interest with the National Capital Planning Commission, and with the Smithsonian Institution it shares an interest in the city's history. The primary function of the Commission of Fine Arts, however, lies in the area of aesthetics. Its aim is to secure the highest standards of design for the structures and landscaping plans which fall under its purview, and to consider carefully the relationship of these structures and landscapes to the areas—and particularly the historic structures—that surround them. The Commission of Fine Arts is the aesthetic "watchdog" of the Nation's Capital, and its historical exercise of this role has had a large part in bringing to reality the ambitious plans for the federal city which this exhibition documents.

J. Carter Brown, *Chairman*, THE COMMISSION OF FINE ARTS

National Capital Planning Commission

The history of the National Capital, while in part an echo of the historical drama enacted in other American cities, is also unique. For Washington has always been a special place where national government interests and local government interests are joined in a federal-municipal partnership. It is the responsibility of the National Capital Planning Commission to support this partnership and at the same time ensure that national government needs and priorities are satisfactorily resolved.

Washington is also a laboratory, a special place where new ideas about cities can be tested in the crucible of daily municipal operations. The National Capital has always attracted promoters of innovative ideas and concepts, precisely because it is in some sense a model for the rest of the nation. Plans and proposals depicted in the Federal City Exhibition amply illustrate the variety and range of thought applied to this city.

During this Bicentennial year we mark the two hundredth birthday of our nation and the fiftieth anniversary of the establishment of the National Capital Planning Commission as the comprehensive planning agency for the Nation's Capital. Moreover, the Smithsonian Institution and the Commission of Fine Arts, which have joined the Planning Commission in sponsoring this exhibition, have also been intimately involved in the history of this city. Recognizing Washington's special character and gaining an understanding of how the city has been planned and developed are appropriate aspects of the Bicentennial celebration—and the goals of this exhibition.

Charles H. Conrad, *Executive Director*
NATIONAL CAPITAL PLANNING COMMISSION

THE HISTORY

WASHINGTON PANORAMA

A brief view of the planned Capital City

FREDERICK GUTHEIM, AIP

Consultant, National Capital Planning Commission

The Washington Plan

TO MOVE THROUGH THE STREETS OF WASHINGTON IS TO EXPERIENCE THE POWER-ful geometry of the city's plan. Its system of radial avenues reinforces the heights of the land, further defined by public buildings of the capital city. The ideal architecture of domes, obelisks, temples, towers is more than a sky-line; it is a series of vantage points, visual references, reinforcing each other with reciprocal views along carefully planned sight lines. A mile and a half separates the Capitol from the White House, so the city is unified over vast distances, often seeming to anticipate the speed and directness of the motor car in the plan of two centuries ago.

The Washington plan has been called the last of the late Renaissance or baroque city plans of the western world, but it is correctly regarded as of neoclassical origin in the late eighteenth century. The circles and radial streets of the 1696 plan of Annapolis more properly express the characteris-tics of the baroque city, to be distinguished from the gridiron plan seen, for example, in Philadelphia. The planner of Washington's monumental core, Pierre Charles L'Enfant, was a gifted interpreter of the landscape designer Lenôtre, a planner of Versailles. But above all, L'Enfant was the creature of his time, a century of princely creations, of spectacle, of rational humanism and revolution, of urban visions and cities of space and motion that spoke in the language of classical absolutism. Washington was by far the largest, the most ambitious of the western world's new capital cities—appropriate to the nation's continental scope and future. It was not, however, the paradox of democratic intention it has been claimed to be. Rather, it expressed a peak in the aspirations of the new republic.

What is commonly referred to as "the L'Enfant Plan" embraces not only the initial design of the French engineer, but its transposition by the surveyor Andrew Ellicott into the first official map of the city; the 1803 plats by the city surveyor Nicholas King; various building regulations, by George Wash-ington and others, to implement the plan; and the various documents, par-ticularly the "manuscript map," that were drawn by L'Enfant and illustrate his intentions, permitting more detailed interpretation of his basic design. This body of material should be regarded in its totality. (On this and other reference materials, see the bibliographical notes, pp. 69-72.)

The city L'Enfant planned survived its initial misfortunes; it persisted over the growth and change of the nineteenth century to achieve a new apprecia-tion and recognition in the planning renaissance of 1900. The remarkable dynamism and vitality to which the city owes its present character and ap-pearance seems most traceable to the shrewd topographical realism of the plan: its management of streams, drainage, and river frontages, and its recog-nition of ridges, terraces, and, most of all, strategic heights of land which were to become the sites of major public buildings. Once L'Enfant's plan as translated by innumerable official and administrative acts had been established—the sites acquired as public reservations, the street plan laid out on the ground and city lots platted and sold—the continuity of L'Enfant's conception was assured and would survive even the great changes brought by nineteenth-century building size and scale as well as urban technology. In the late nineteenth century, the city began to grow beyond L'Enfant's plan. A new metropolitan framework would ultimately be required. For a long time, however, indeed until the mid-twentieth century, the L'Enfant Plan itself provided the most powerful inspiration for efforts to extend and reinterpret the original design intentions in the light of contemporary needs.

1790-1800 Designing the City

The selection of the capital's site along the Potomac followed nearly fifteen years of caravan-style government that moved from city to city. Even in the Residence Act of 16 July 1790, a wide range of possible locations along the river was specified. President Washington was familiar with the entire region from the Chesapeake to its source in the Appalachians and the western territory beyond, but the site at the confluence of the Potomac with the Eastern Branch held several advantages. Like the site of the ancient capital city of England, this spot was at the head of navigation, accessible and open to a flourishing sea trade, and yet protected by being two hundred miles inland, far enough to offer strategic defense against sea attack. The beckoning West could soon be made accessible by river and canal. The location downriver allowed for immediate access to the vast and rich coastal hinterland. At the fall line, water power was available. George Washington's personal sentiments may be inferred: the spot was near Mount Vernon and its urban reference, the bustling port city of Alexandria, which could be viewed from the "President's Palace." The original boundaries of the City of Washington encompassed a ten-mile square, specified by the 1790 act, and included a portion of Virginia.

Pierre L'Enfant was a familiar figure to the leaders of the new nation, having redesigned Federal Hall in New York City in 1789 as a temporary headquarters for the Congress. Born in France into a family of artists, he had no doubt visited that country's outstanding contributions to garden and city design, Versailles, Chantilly, and the Tuileries Gardens, before embarking for America as a young engineer officer to aid the colonists' cause. The creator of these seventeenth-century French masterpieces, André Lenôtre, applied

FIGURE 1. *First Published Plan of Washington, 1792. This "small version" published by Thackara and Vallance of Philadelphia shows the part of the peninsula planned by L'Enfant. The dark lines in the southwest quadrant denote the canal system intended to tie the Potomac River to the Eastern Branch (the Anacostia River) through the heart of the city. Sites for major public buildings and markets are indicated. Diagonal avenues slice across an irregularly spaced grid, allowing for subordination of the "inter-stices" to the major focal points. The long "public walk" (later the Mall), south of the canal, connecting the Capitol with the proposed memorial to George Washington; the ceremonial avenue connecting the Capitol with the President's House; and the short leg between the memorial and the President's House form the monumental triangle around which much of the early settlement of Washington would occur.*

Courtesy Library of Congress.

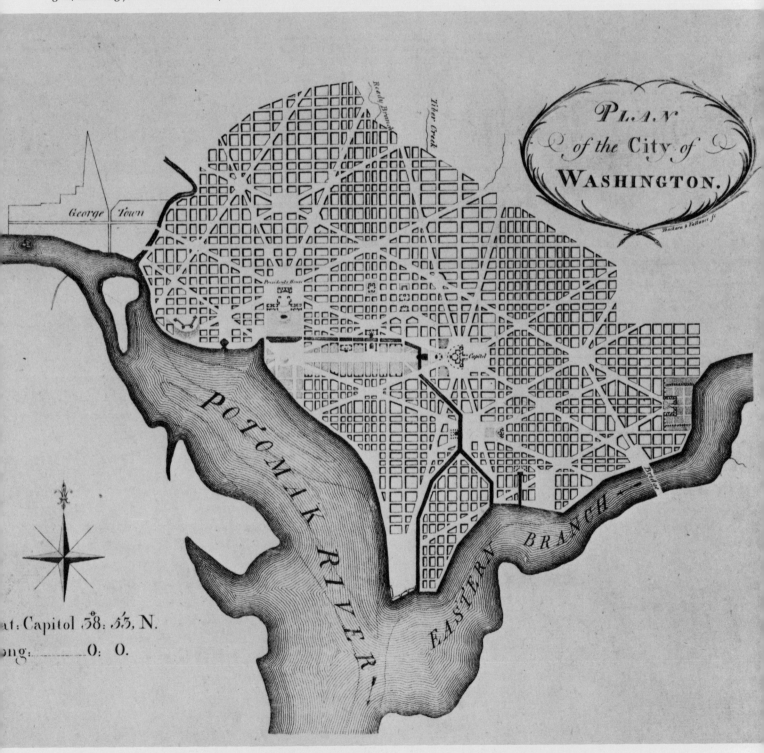

3

engineering to landscape design, enabling the construction of elaborate waterworks, the planning of complicated terraces, and the grading of land with new accuracy. Lenôtre's basic principles of garden design as revealed in his work—the importance of site, light, and life—were equally applicable to larger citywide schemes. Thus, L'Enfant, having never before designed a city, but being an acute observer of Lenôtre's creations and their contemporary urban expressions, was able to apply the same basic principles on the banks of the Potomac (figure 1).

Instructed by President Washington to survey the site and sketch locations for public buildings in the peninsular flatlands and terraces between the Eastern Branch of the Potomac and Georgetown, L'Enfant reconnoitered the land on horseback. The natural topography in these boundaries offered several critical features available for inclusion and embellishment. To the east rose Jenkins Hill (later Capitol Hill), to the west a small terrace. The broad Tiber Creek—a typical Potomac tidal inlet—cut straight across the site, becoming a smaller rushing stream north of Jenkins Hill. Along the Eastern Branch the water was deep enough for navigation, with several fingers of land scalloping the south shore of the peninsula. The embryonic settlement of Carrollsburg already occupied one of these Eastern Branch fingers, with further commercial competition to the west in the form of the just-platted "paper town" of Hamburg and the thriving port city of George-town. Downstream lay the older city of Alexandria (figure 2).

As if envisioning the elaborate water system employed in Lenôtre's Chan-tilly whereby the river Nonnette was transformed into a canal parallel to the main terrace, L'Enfant suggested that one of Washington's important features be a canal, in this case the major drainage and trade artery being created from the Tiber Creek. (The name of this stream was already a century old, deriving from the old plantation "Rome," but it reflected perfectly the neoclassical enthusiasm of the Revolutionary period.) For his canal to the Potomac, L'Enfant drew the main branch as extending from the foot of Jenkins Hill and branching out south of his envisioned Civic Center to two points along the Eastern Branch. Although the extent of the canal held the promise of flourishing trade to benefit many parts of the city, the waterway was both an essential means of draining the flood plains of the proposed low-lying urban center, and also an element of a vast picturesque waterworks scheme. As Versailles's magnificent spectacle of fountains was connected to the drainage of flatlands and the fulfillment of its Grand Canal, so—L'Enfant suggested—water from the Tiber could create a large cascade rolling down Jenkins Hill and discharging itself into the canal and the Potomac.

FIGURE 2. *The L'Enfant Plan in Its Larger Context, 1793. A topographical survey made by Andrew Ellicott of the prescribed ten-mile square defines the flat basin land covered by L'Enfant's design. The proximity of this site to the port cities of Alexandria (lower right corner) and Georgetown is also delineated as is the general orientation of the L'Enfant plan to natural and man-made waterways. The surrounding hills are varied by the tributaries of the Potomac. This natural topography gives the city its special identity, re-inforced later on by the strategic placement of federal installations and the establishment of the city's park system.*

Courtesy Library of Congress.

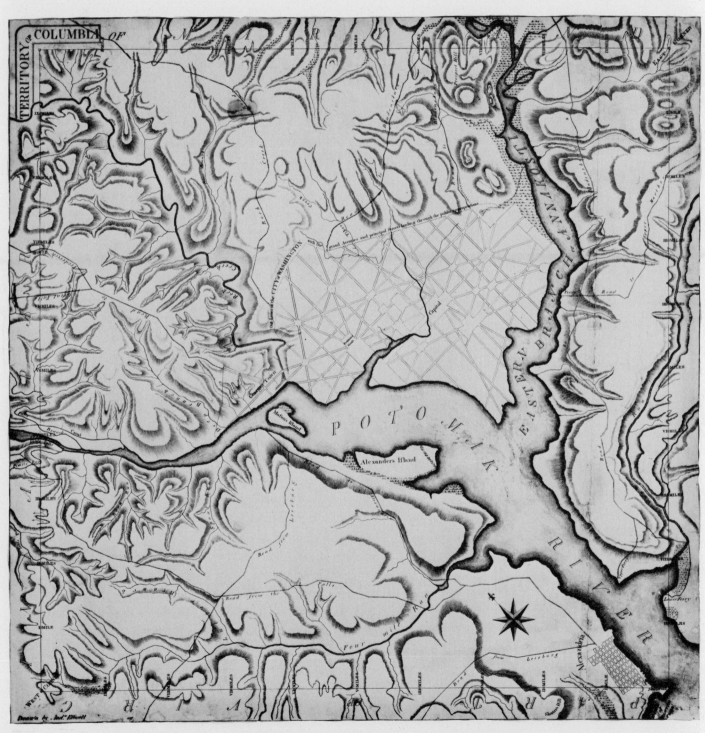

In designing the new city's street system, L'Enfant asked the secretary of state, Thomas Jefferson, to lend him maps of European cities which Jefferson had studied during his travels. Access to these plans in no way compromised the brilliant originality of L'Enfant's plan. Among these maps were those of Karlsruhe and Saint Petersburg, the latter city designed by the Frenchman LeBlond for Peter the Great—historically an important exercise in baroque urban design. As this city plan reinforced L'Enfant's recollections of the famous garden plan of Versailles, he designated the land south and parallel to the west branch of the canal as a "public walk," the "Grand Avenue" (later the Mall), with the Congress House placed on Jenkins Hill and connected by the city's most important diagonal avenue to the President's House on the western terrace. The major east-west axis, created by the Congress House and the Mall, met the shorter north-south axis of the President's House at a point envisioned by L'Enfant to display a river-front equestrian statue commemorating President Washington. Other features of L'Enfant's plan derived from this monumental right-angled triangle and were complementary.

The axial theme enunciated by the Grand Avenue and the President's House recurred throughout the city. A cross axis extending along Eighth Street, halfway between the President's House and the Congress House, stretched southward from the proposed nonsectarian National Church through the turning basin of the canal and its attendant markets to the canal terminus on the banks of the Potomac River, where the site for the Naval Column was provided. (This extensive avenue recalled the long view Lenôtre cut through the Tuileries Gardens—figure 40—from the Louvre to the site of the Arc de Triomphe and beyond.) Along this cross axis may have been L'Enfant's site for the judiciary function, although his aim is obscure and a good case has been made for an alternative location at what is now Judiciary Square.

Attention has focused almost exclusively on the fine arts origins of the L'Enfant Plan. Important as are these roots in Paris and Versailles and the landscape tradition of Lenôtre, L'Enfant also knew the scientific and engineering traditions of the eighteenth century. In reflecting these traditions with their characteristic absolutism and integrity, L'Enfant's plan could not have derived from the political structure of the United States; more probably it derived from science, and especially mathematics. Both the street plan, with the suggestion of Cartesian coordinates in its gridiron layout, and the persistent neoclassicism were warmly reflective of Descartes's view of architecture and planning.

Anticipating the rapid growth of the city commensurate with the country's growth, L'Enfant planned for strategic urban development to be generated simultaneously from a number of points marked by major buildings and keyed to the markets fronting the canal and the business district, which he intended should lie along the major east-west avenue between the Congress House and the Eastern Branch. As if designating these points of growth, he drew several squares well distributed throughout the city. However flourishing these settlements were to become, they revolved about the central triangle of governmental and cultural life. The major diagonal, later Pennsylvania Avenue, was to be lined with playhouses, rooms for assembly, academies, and other places of diversion, while the Grand Avenue, later called the Mall, was to hold villas suitable for ambassadorial residences. A richly textured cosmopolitan life characteristic of a capital city was clearly envisioned and provided for in L'Enfant's grand plan.

The Port City 1800-1860

Clearly L'Enfant's visions overestimated both the nation's own immediate resources and its early commitment to the particular settlement as the national city. His efforts to promote his plan of Washington were rejected and he was dismissed—and later formally resigned. Yet by 1800, as the government moved into the new city, an unfinished President's House (figure 3) and a Capitol Building placed a seemingly interminable mile and a half apart had nevertheless been established as primary indicators of L'Enfant's grand scheme. Stretching across the flatlands horizon, the major streets as laid out by the designer as far north as Boundary Street (now Florida Avenue) would remain, with major changes in his plan occurring in the siting of public buildings and the use of both the Grand Avenue and the secondary avenues and adjacent land.

American figures like Franklin and Jefferson, and those like Joel Barlow who appeared in early Washington, were at home in the age whether in Europe or the United States. It was to such as these that L'Enfant's plan recommended itself, not to the more popular elements of society.

In its first half century, the city's environment was profoundly and adversely affected by the deforestation and increased settlement along the Potomac River upstream. Severe silting of the city's river front occurred. The river's edge gave way to an indeterminate marsh, often flooding as far north as Pennsylvania Avenue at high water and carrying in its wake the sewage discharged into the sluggish Tiber Creek. The river subjected the lowlands city as a whole to severe environmental hazards. In the summer months, the heat and sickly conditions of the marshes forced many residents to higher land and led the affluent to seek permanent residences there, leaving to the transient and the poor the lowlands residential areas in amongst the industrial areas of the port and other services. Still, improvements and extensions were made to the city—despite the unhealthy conditions and the fact that although officially established, L'Enfant's plan lacked detail and force. Much of the plan's persistence over the next century depended on piecemeal decisions.

The British-born architect Benjamin Latrobe arrived in Washington in 1802, being commissioned by President Jefferson to advise him on a drydocks scheme for the Navy Yard. In the following year, Latrobe began the completion of the Capitol (figure 71). Observing the lack of a visual connection between the long axis of the Mall and the west front of the Capitol, Latrobe planned an impressive flight of stairs leading up the hill from the lower land.

Work on the strategic canal along which the future city would develop got under way with the incorporation of a canal company in 1802. The versatile Latrobe worked on this project as well as on the Capitol, bowing to economic stringencies throughout the next decade. Wood was used as lining for the city canal and locks. Almost as quickly as the canal was constructed, it fell apart. In 1811, one of the locks was destroyed by a severe storm. Five years later, other locks and the lining were tumbled down or washed away. The failure of the Washington Canal to live up to its expectations was due in part to the indecisiveness of the federal government to commit necessary funds for the project. Local sectional differences also weakened the enterprise, as Georgetown and Alexandria wished for no additional rivals in the battle for sea commerce, and the turnpike interests were fighting any moves to siphon off land trade.

With the formation of the Chesapeake & Ohio Canal Company in 1828, attention focused once again on Washington's ailing and shallow city canal. The long-anticipated C & O Canal was carved out from Georgetown westward to Harpers Ferry and beyond. From Georgetown the canal extended to Seventeenth and B Streets where it joined the city canal. Alexandria found a role in this scheme with an aqueduct bridge constructed just west of Georgetown to carry the Virginia traffic southward. By 1843 the C & O Canal was completed from the first range of the Appalachians to the Washington Canal connection.

Simultaneously with the C & O Canal's inception began the railroad, here most notably the Baltimore & Ohio, which in 1835 had linked itself to Washington over the angry protests of both canal and turnpike interests. The

FIGURE 3. *The Bucolic City, ca. 1803. The President's House located in the distance and Blodgett's Hotel (used as the Post Office) on the far right at Eighth Street are separated in this drawing by reminders of the city's sylvan origins. The clearing and platting of the site and the laying of streets was a slow and gradual process. During the nineteenth century, farm animals and a more clearly stated topography occupied the foreground of a rising monumental and urbanized backdrop.* Courtesy Library of Congress.

later arrival of the railroad in Washington signaled the decline of new canal schemes. By mid-century the railroad tracks had invaded the city, and by the Civil War the intracity streetcar system had begun. For seventy-five years the city would have to live with the railroad, with its grade crossings, smoke, noise, and visual disfigurement of parks and monumental areas of the capital: a continually expanding and threatening nuisance, but a vital public service.

Although land traffic facilitated by rails began to dominate the Washington landscape, the river continued to bustle with trade, especially along the

Eastern Branch (figure 4). The river still possessed abundant fisheries, a resource that had supported aboriginal settlements and astonished the earliest white explorers in the area. In the 1830s, the Potomac and its tributaries counted one hundred and fifty fisheries. Farmers from Maryland, Pennsylvania, and Virginia transported their produce to Washington and took away large quantities of fish. The supply of some fish was so plentiful that they were used on nearby farms as fertilizer. A testimony to this now-lost wealth is indicated by the naming of Buzzard Point along the Eastern Branch, likely a site where these scavengers fed off the dead fish washed ashore.

While private interests were left to develop the commercial city largely on their own, the government planned and did make major improvements to the city's ceremonial core. The Mall early fell into separate jurisdictions and thus presented a "patchquilt" appearance (figure 39). The Botanic Gardens, enlarged in 1842 with a collection of exotic botanical specimens from the Wilkes Arctic Exploring Expedition, was situated at the foot of Capitol Hill. A virtual plant and tree museum for many decades, it suffered from what Architect of the Capitol Edward Clark described, in 1882, as the "lack of an intelligent public interest in the scientific objects of a botanical gardens, and an excess of interest in its adventitious and recreative incidents."

The Botanic Gardens received a cultural bolster when, in 1846, the Smithsonian Institution was established seven blocks to the west. The construction of James Renwick's Norman-styled Smithsonian Building (figure 37) stimulated moves to design the Mall grounds in a romantic style suited to this new turreted architecture.

In 1850, Washington financier William Corcoran suggested to Joseph Henry, Secretary of the Smithsonian, and to President Millard Fillmore that the nationally renowned landscape gardener Andrew Jackson Downing be commissioned to design the grounds for the Mall as well as the parks north and south of the President's House (figure 5). In the written portion of his plan, Downing set out three objectives: to form a "National Park," to provide an influential example of the "natural style of landscape gardening," and to create a "public museum of living trees and shrubs." In the graphic plan, he drew up a scheme of connecting curvilinear walks, filled in with trees, pleasure grounds, and fountains. The Mall would be joined to the city to the north by new bridges of design appropriate to the romantic tract. The sharp bend of the canal made in the reservation named "Fountain Park" fronting Seventh Street was shifted in a smooth diagonal toward the north along Missouri Avenue, adding to commercial sites but defining additional land for park purposes. Like L'Enfant, Downing envisioned water displays

FIGURE 4. *The River City, 1834. A view of the city from the heights of rural Anacostia reveals the waterways as the dominant traffic arteries of the antebellum city. The Potomac (to the far left) and the Eastern Branch (in the foreground) are busy with sailing vessels. The Navy Yard on the west bank of the Eastern Branch is denoted in this painting by the large covered structure around which workers' houses are clustered. Above, on the summit of Jenkins Hill, the Capitol Building looks over the basin city toward the Presi-* *dent's House farther west. The route of Pennsylvania Avenue is traced by the straight line of houses linking the two major public buildings in the landscape.* *Courtesy National Archives.*

as critical to the aesthetic fulfillment of the city. Under Downing's plan, Fountain Park would be supplied from a basin in the Capitol, its overflow directed to the pond to be carved out.

Downing's scheme was too extensive for the nation's purse and commitment, however, and his untimely death in 1852 left the Smithsonian grounds as the only immediate beneficiary of the plan. Described by Downing as "thickly planted with the rarest trees and shrubs, to give greater seclusion and beauty to its immediate precincts," the Smithsonian grounds remained a powerful and much-admired design ideal for Washington's park system as a

FIGURE 5. *Andrew Jackson Downing's Plan for Laying Out the Mall and the President's Park, 1851. The separate public reservations along the Mall are joined by winding roadways and by proximity to the canal. In this plan, each major section retains a distinct identity, defined by the major structures it embellishes. From left to right, the six "different and distinct scenes" include the Botanic Gardens, Fountain Park, Smithsonian Park or "Pleasure Grounds," Evergreen Garden, Monument Park, and the President's Park.*

From the Annual Report of the Army Corps of Engineers, October 1867.

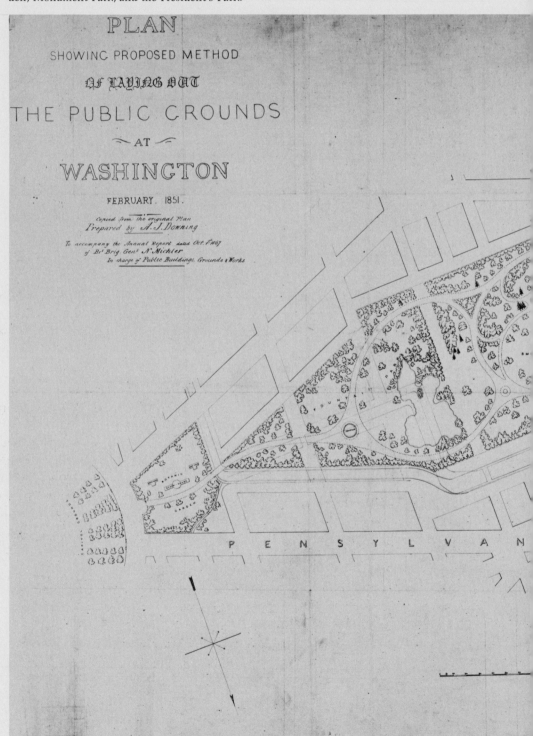

whole—especially after the Civil War, when L'Enfant's neighborhood park-lets were finally realized. The Mall persisted as an unrelated chain of separate parks until the early twentieth century, although many landscape architects and engineers such as Frederick Law Olmsted and Major Nathaniel Michler were to argue otherwise in the city's post–Civil War era.

As the concept of the Mall evolved from the official residential character proposed by L'Enfant's plan into a cultural-institutional center surrounded by public parks, the functions of other parts of the city were altered as well, largely by the increasingly fortuitous placement of public buildings. British-educated George Hadfield, architect of the brick and white-porticoed depart-mental buildings originally flanking the President's House, designed in 1820 a City Hall for Washington. L'Enfant imagined the municipal center as developing to the east of the south branch of the Washington Canal, far enough from the federal functions to assert municipal independence, but near enough to the port-industrial area and major arteries to play an integral part in the life of the city.

As a dramatic step away from this intention, Hadfield's City Hall was located a few blocks northwest of the Capitol at Fourth and D Streets and served as the first element of a sprawling municipal center in the district now called Judiciary Square. (On his original plan L'Enfant had identified this relatively high site—at the focus of two short radial avenues, today both named Indiana Avenue—to serve some monumental function, although he did not elaborate further.) In contrast to the ornate and painstaking work on both the President's House and the Congress House, City Hall was a monu-ment to economy in public architecture. The interiors were described as "almost barnlike in absolute simplicity," while the exterior displayed a restrained Greek Ionic portico flanked by two wings. This quiet building remained unheralded in public architecture through the more flamboyant years of the post–Civil War era, gaining stronger recognition in the early twentieth century as it anticipated the revival of classical taste.

Another Hadfield-designed building, the Treasury, was consumed by fire, and it was the need for a new building in 1834 that wrought a crucial change upon the L'Enfant Plan. Robert Mills, Latrobe's protégé, designed the Ionic-styled Treasury Building for the site on Pennsylvania Avenue, blocking out the view from the Capitol of the President's House. This "spoliation" of a carefully designed terminus to the city's major diagonal avenue was sup-posedly instigated by President Andrew Jackson. The Treasury's siting, while deplored by some contemporaries as well as by later generations of city planners, followed a pattern set as far back as the government's occupation of the city—a pattern of lack of enforcement of any over-all plan for the public spaces, and especially for sites and designs of public buildings. The uncertainties of congressional appropriation produced a much smaller Treasury Building than Mills had anticipated. Additions were required to complete the structure, this time under supervision of the architect Thomas U. Walter.

During Mills's considerable period as architect of public buildings (1836–51), he designed other public edifices in the city. On the square bounded by F and G Streets, between Seventh and Ninth Streets, NW, L'Enfant had specified a nonsectarian National Church. In 1836, however, work began at that site on the Patent Office Building, supervised by Mills. Where the worship of God was thus replaced by the worship of technology, a powerful Doric portico fronted F Street, with a clear vista down Eighth Street to the Center Market facing the canal and southward to the banks of the Potomac. In fact, if a viewer stood in front of the Patent Office—now the National Portrait Gallery—he could still grasp L'Enfant's intentions for a broad street complete with a compelling visual experience.

One block from the Patent Office, at the corner of Eighth and E Streets, NW, Mills designed the Corinthian-styled Post Office Building. The location of the Post Office on this site was more a matter of tradition than deliberate planning, as it was formerly occupied by Blodgett's Hotel (see figure 3) which the government rented for its postal functions. By 1855, the new building was extended northward to F Street, again under the guidance of the architect Walter.

Through the first two decades of the nineteenth century, the city's population was concentrated in the low-lying areas along Pennsylvania Avenue and in a few smaller scattered locations. The ridge followed by F Street was the northern limit of the main settlement. Water was supplied by many private springs, but a public supply was furnished by City Spring (Sixth and C Streets); Caffey's Spring (Ninth and F Streets); Franklin Square Spring, early connected by a pipeline to provide the White House water supply; and Smith Spring, which furnished water to the Capitol and the adjacent parts of Pennsylvania Avenue. These numerous springs proved inadequate to a growing population, and the city actually experienced several major fires against which this limited water supply was clearly inadequate. The need for a new water system was in fact so great that when—by 1853—the Army engineer Montgomery Meigs reported on the feasibility of a water system originating at Great Falls, Congress appropriated the largest outlay of public money for the city since it had appropriated funds for its own Capitol. This design of the water system originating in Great Falls, Maryland, made it clear to the city that it needed access to the resources of a much larger area than the ten-mile square specified in 1790. A request was posed to the Maryland legislature to grant the United States a right of way through Maryland territory along the Potomac. When all the land needed for the conduit had been condemned, construction began and continued—with many interruptions caused by on-and-off congressional appropriations—until the system's completion during the Civil War.

Water diverted from Great Falls was conveyed to the receiving reservoir near Little Falls at Dalecarlia. From the Dalecarlia Reservoir, the settled water was carried to the distributing reservoir in Georgetown whence it was piped to the users. In securing this nearly twelve-mile-long connection, Meigs designed the famous single-arched masonry Cabin John Bridge to carry the conduit over the Cabin John Valley, as well as the Pennsylvania Avenue Bridge at Georgetown which by a series of cast-iron pipes carried water over Rock Creek. Meigs's system proved not to provide consistently clear water, but its supply was abundant and its essential elements served the city well into the twentieth century.

This adequate water supply—one of the first among American cities—brought the city up to modern standards. In Washington's case, the supply also had an important effect on the configurations of residential neighborhoods. Since the water reached Georgetown and the northwest quadrant first, before being piped to the rest of the city, those northwest sections were more desirable as residential areas, whereas neighborhoods east of the Capitol were periodically threatened with a water shortage, as occurred in 1889. Thus, as the city grew, the affluent clustered in the higher, western areas having the predictable water supply while the less affluent were relegated to the poorly serviced areas of the lower city. This distribution of economic classes was abetted by many other contributing factors, and the configuration persists to this day.

By the 1860s Washington's population had largely settled (figure 6) between the Capitol and the President's House and north of Pennsylvania Avenue, all within walking distance of the government offices and the business district. The President's House and the nearby embassies set the residential tone of the area. An indicator of thriving residential function was the fact that a large percentage of new churches constructed in the city were located in this area. Other thick settlements formed about the Navy Yard in the southeast quadrant of the city, along Pennsylvania Avenue between the President's House and Georgetown, as well as in Georgetown itself. The port

FIGURE 6. *Boschke Topographical Map of the District of Columbia, 1861. The darkened sections of the original plan indicate major concentrations of settlement. The streets shown in the unsettled areas were likely nonexistent in 1861, but their appearance on paper promised the retention of L'Enfant's street plan through the nineteenth century. The rural surroundings dominating the appearance of the District are joined with the urbanized portion by the railroad through the northeast, the Chesapeake & Ohio Canal along the Potomac in the northwest, several bridges between the District and the Virginia shore, and the various highways presaging major arteries in the future city.*

Courtesy Library of Congress.

TOPOGRAPHICAL
Map
OF THE
DISTRICT OF COLUMBIA
SURVEYED
IN THE YEARS 1856 '57 '58 & '59
BY
A. BOSCHKE.

Published by
D. MCCLELLAND, BLANCHARD & MOHUN
WASHINGTON, D.C.
1861

city, rising rapidly from the river front to high ground, offered escape from the unhealthy lowlands. By the 1830s, the residential area was only a short ride from the business district—stretching out along Pennsylvania Avenue, beginning at the front of Capitol Hill and gradually pushing westward to Fourteenth Street—by the omnibus line first established between Georgetown and the Navy Yard. In distinction from the crowded row-house residential patterns of the post–Civil War era, the residential lots of Washington were spacious, offering ample room for large gardens. In fact, "the cultivated gardens and lawns about the houses in Washington were regarded as one of the distinctive features of the city," according to historian Wilhelmus Bryan.

L'Enfant's original planned area, framed by Boundary Street (now Florida Avenue), well contained the antebellum city. Much of the land within the planned area had actually not been developed, although the street scheme remained in force, at least on maps. Open fields and unplanned settlements merged into the open countryside beyond Boundary Street. Still, even prior to the Civil War boom, faint stirrings of suburban development *within* the District of Columbia could be observed. Such an organized settlement, at a distance from the center, was Uniontown. Directly across the Eastern Branch from the Navy Yard (figure 4), Uniontown was laid out in 1854 as Washington's first actual suburban development. The establishment of the Baltimore & Ohio Railroad drew in office workers from farther afield than the walking perimeters of the city. Several already established streets, incorporated in the L'Enfant planned city, now stretched into the adjacent countryside beyond.

1860-1865 The Civil War

The Civil War, as decisive to the capital city as to the nation, transformed Washington from a thriving village into a bustling city—with a streetcar railroad system and suburban growth—that could respond to the war emergency conditions on a metropolitan basis. In serving as a receiving depot for recruits, the city absorbed a startling rise in population that flooded its hotels and rooming houses. Temporary camp structures were erected beyond L'Enfant's boundaries to the north. Extant buildings and grounds were endowed with new functions: the basement of the Capitol served as a bakery, and cattle were slaughtered on the grounds to the south of the President's House. Other buildings were turned into hospitals (figure 7) and military headquarters. Entire tent cities appeared. But beyond providing mere physical accommodation to the transient militia and swelled ranks of civil servants,

FIGURE 7. *Military Hospital and Encampment in Mount Pleasant, 1861–65. A former site of antebellum country living, Mount Pleasant became a major cluster of military hospitals and encampments during the Civil War. The site's location north of Boundary Street (now Florida Avenue) previewed the trend of later suburban growth.*
Courtesy Library of Congress.

the city became itself a symbol of the nation's unity, especially in the completion of the extended Capitol and its huge dome (see figure 9).

At the outbreak of the war, the city was threatened by Confederate forces. Great uneasiness prevailed. In a few months' time, however, thousands of Union troops had moved in, bringing a revived sense of security. Various physical developments followed to enforce protection of the city. A chain of fortifications encircling the city were constructed on commanding hills in the county of Washington and through nearby Virginia (figure 8). Barracks, encampments, hospital tent cities, and vast areas turned over to horses, forage, provisions, military equipment, and supplies were seen everywhere. Several bridges and ferries connected the peninsular city with the Virginia

19

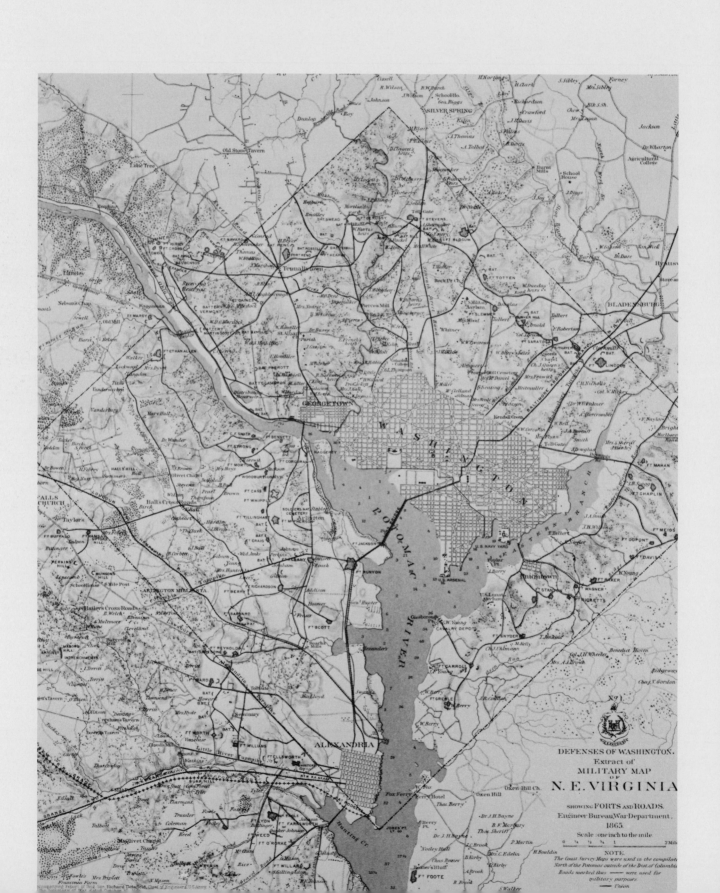

FIGURE 8. *The Defenses of Washington, 1865.*
The ring of forts linking the District and the
Virginia locations indicate the high points
of land overlooking the basin city. This tying
together of the area's resources in a common
effort predicted the later metropolitan city.
Courtesy Library of Congress.

shore, tightening the links between city and countryside. With the city and its environs secure, the government concentrated the production of food in the affected areas of Maryland and Virginia, diverting these Virginia counties away from a Richmond orientation and toward Washington. As demonstrated by Meigs's water supply system, the city relied on the resources of the larger area, anticipating metropolitan solutions to Washington's needs. And as the wartime city gained self-sufficiency within this well-defined larger area, manufactories sprang up, intensifying in the local area the supply of food-related goods.

The spread of the military population to the highlands beyond Boundary Street outstretched the ability and willingness of residents to walk the increasing distances between home and work. The "walking city" could no longer be contained by the pressures of sheer physical growth. In 1862, the first streetcar railroad was chartered: soon it would emancipate the old river-bottom city, allowing for residential areas to be significantly separated from work. The expansion of this transportation system ushered in the street-car suburb, heralding the physical and social configurations of the postwar era.

The wartime boom city also exhibited expansion and change in the business district. Pennsylvania Avenue as the city's primary commercial street waned while F Street established itself—after the 1870s—as a new and desirable shopping area. A major element in L'Enfant's plan, Pennsylvania Avenue was now increasingly relegated to the marginal commercial interests. From the south side of the avenue to the city canal, various forms of entertainment developed, reflecting the impact on Washington of the transient military population. Populated by prostitutes, gamblers, and a criminal element, the triangle formed by the two major axes isolated itself socially from the rest of the city, defying attempts at redemption until the end of the century when construction of the new Post Office Building presaged the area's occupation by public buildings.

Symbolizing Washington's stature as a mature city able to accommodate its physical profile to the emergencies of war—and acknowledging its stature thus as a capital city worthy of the nation—a new skyline landmark appeared in the extensions to the Capitol. Commencing in 1851, Thomas U. Walter designed new north and south wings to the building, the newly enlarged base to be crowned with a much magnified cast-iron dome (figure 9) replacing that of wood designed by Charles Bulfinch (figure 72). In the completion, Washington gained fulfillment of the monumental requisites of L'Enfant's plans for Jenkins Hill, described by him in 1791 as "a pedestal waiting for a monument." This dramatically augmented public building would serve as the home of a reunited Congress and the beckoner of new representatives from western states.

1865-1900 The Postbellum City

After the Union's fate had been decided, Congress faced anew the problem of its commitment to Washington as the nation's capital. The city had served the government well as a military headquarters and encampment, but could its physical appearance satisfy the luxurious postwar expectations of the gilded age? Clearly there was little at hand to figure forth a city representative of the vast country that would soon stretch from ocean to ocean. The Washington Canal—planned to serve as a major transportation, communication, and aesthetic artery—served more as a barrier between the ceremonial avenue and the Mall, and was a notorious receptacle for the city's sewage. The fetid canal was joined on the south to the noxious Potomac flats which were periodically flooded by the river itself. The Mall, transformed from a residential avenue to a "patchquilt" park setting for public buildings (figure 76), suffered from irregular maintenance by the many agencies and bureaus responsible for it and its most unsatisfactory termination at the marshy river front. Barely rising above these unhealthy and often unsightly public properties, the President's House inspired repeated conjectures about its possible removal to higher ground in the healthier countryside.

Before the Civil War, public and private interests had taken it upon themselves to escape from the miasmic lowlands. This process was intensified in the postbellum era. In the thirty-five postwar years, however, the lowlands city was made livable. The city canal was filled in. Streets were paved. The Potomac flats were reclaimed as an integral element in flood-proofing the city. By the end of the century, this vast lowlands area was occupied mainly by public functions, while in the areas beyond, residential development had become fully entrenched.

In shaping the postbellum city, four groups of men were influential: *1)* the Board of Public Works set up under the brief *territorial* form of government; *2)* the Army Corps of Engineers, which in 1867 was entrusted with the federal interests in the physical development of the city; *3)* designers, often of national recognition, commissioned by the government for specific projects; and *4)* the local designers, developers, and financiers who endowed the city with uniquely "Washington" buildings and neighborhoods.

Alexander Shepherd, member of the short-lived Board of Public Works, was the most celebrated figure in the physical improvement of the city. Washington-born and deeply committed to the city as "worthy of the nation," Shepherd led a vigorous work force, covering the ruinous city canal and converting it into a street. Sewers were laid and streets graded, paved, and planted with trees. Markets that had developed spontaneously and contrary to the intentions of L'Enfant's system of open spaces were summarily removed; the "reservations" L'Enfant's plan had established were restored to their original purposes.

Concentrating on the most visible section of the city, its downtown and nearby western areas, Shepherd consequently reinforced the neglect of the eastern and southern neighborhoods. Moreover, the enormous unauthorized debt accumulated by his works over the years 1871 to 1874, and the financial benefits reaped by his friends in the process, invited discredit on Shepherd. Although he was himself driven from government service, Shepherd—one of the city's most fervent advocates—had impressed the Congress as well as visiting dignitaries with the potential grandeur of the city, quashing talk then of removing the federal government to a new midwestern location. And Shepherd's work was impressively continued by the municipal government after the Board of Public Works was disbanded in 1874.

Public works of a more enduring institutional nature, and marked by the ideas of many talented individuals, were undertaken by the Corps of Engineers, providing Washington with the physical components of a modern city—and often the vision that meshed technology with aesthetics. The Corps's work on maintaining public buildings and grounds in the city of Washington adhered to L'Enfant's plan, especially in the carving of the remaining streets and neighborhood parks within the framework of that original plan. As settlements spilled over the original boundaries into the county of Washington (which was outside municipal limits but still in the District of Columbia) and eventually into the suburban counties of Maryland and Virginia, the Corps adapted its works to a larger area and amplified the original settlement to a regional scale.

Nathaniel Michler, a Civil War hero, was the first engineer to be charged with responsibility for the city's public buildings and grounds after the transfer of authority from municipal to federal hands. His office also received all the records of the municipal commissioner of public works, including the manuscript L'Enfant Plan. Far-sighted beyond some preceding Washington designers, Michler envisioned a vast "National Park" along the winding crevice of Rock Creek, a unified Mall, reclamation of the Potomac flats, and a river front developed to accommodate trade and other commercial activities. Although Michler's actual accomplishments were limited to the clearing of the scattered parklets throughout the city, his proposed program anticipated the major significant projects of the rest of the century. Michler's successor and friend of Shepherd, Orville Babcock, left his mark on the drainage, planting, and adornment of the Washington Monument grounds, Lafayette Square, and several other reservations that made up the Mall.

Later members of the Corps (figure 10) performed the arduous and lengthy work of reclaiming the flats. In the process was created a vast piece of land appended to the Mall, the winding shores of that functional and picturesque water later called the Tidal Basin, and Potomac Park (figure 70). The water system initiated by Meigs was now expanded to increase the amount and quality of the supply, a necessary prerequisite to the growth of the city. Parks and other public reservations inside the District of Columbia were developed, following on the heels of private settlement, and new government

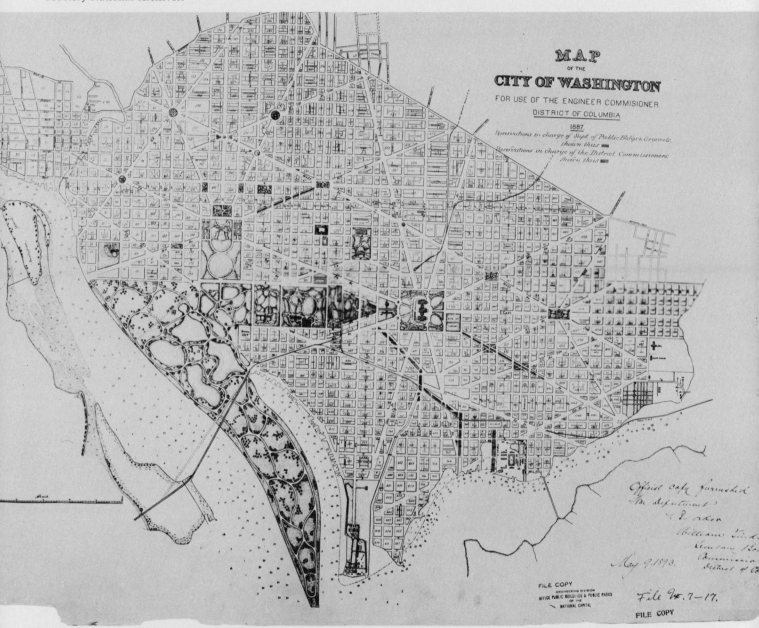

institutions were created—Howard University, the National Zoological Park, and, before the century's end, parcels of land that became Rock Creek Park.

On the other side of the Potomac, although the government had ceded that portion of the District back to the Commonwealth of Virginia in 1846, the Civil War had obliged government occupancy and the construction of forts. After the war, the government not only retained its properties but later expanded them. More visibly, a national cemetery was created with Arlington House as an architectural and historical emblem, the national Valhalla. The Virginia waterfront ultimately mirrored the improving banks on the Washington side. Designating the preserved Mount Vernon as a southernmost terminus, Engineer Peter Hains of the Corps surveyed a route anticipating what is now known as the George Washington Memorial Parkway. And above all, the most highly visible accomplishment of the Corps was the commanding feature of the Washington skyline, the 555-foot-high Washington Monument, an obelisk that had remained half finished (figure 78) since 1855, and was brought to completion by the Army Corps of Engineers in 1885.

The succession of engineers responsible for much of the city's development left a brilliant but unconnected legacy. The improvements appeared piecemeal, unrelated to a comprehensive scheme. Thus, by the end of the century, the city was ripe for a sweeping together of past improvements along with many of the individual suggestions initiated by the territorial government's Board of Public Works and the Corps. This task was envisioned by Colonel Theodore Bingham, whose urban sense had been formed during his service as a military attaché in Berlin and Rome. Bingham urged Congress to improve existing parklands, both as a benefit to city residents and as an inspirational model to park systems in other American cities. Resurrecting L'Enfant's name, Bingham created an atmosphere conducive to congressional and professional action as the city's Centennial neared.

The works of other engineers and architects filled in the landscape created by the military and municipal engineers. Alfred B. Mullett, supervising architect of the Treasury and a contemporary of the energetic Shepherd and Babcock, was commissioned—independently of his official position—to design the new State, War and Navy Building (now known as the Executive Office Building; figure 54) to stand to the west of the President's House. Mullett designed a massive building of majestic qualities, whose cascades of columns signaled both the government's decisive commitment to the future of the city as well as society's preoccupation with the physical symbols of luxury.

Montgomery Meigs, the accomplished officer of the Corps who had designed Washington's water system, was specially invited by several government bureaus to provide designs for public buildings. Most notably, Meigs designed (with Adolph Cluss) the red-bricked National Museum—now the Arts and Industries Building—to house the expanded collections of the

26

FIGURE 11. *The Capitol Grounds Designed by Frederick Law Olmsted, Sr., 1874. The cascading terrace connecting the building with the romantic walks of the Mall (at the bottom of the picture) was designed by Olmsted to resolve the awkward siting of the building slightly over the crest of the hill. The linear grove of trees that obstructed a view of the building as a whole is replaced in this plan by carefully sited clusters of trees intended to focus attention on the building's entirety.*

From *Glenn Brown,* History of the United States Capitol *(Washington, D.C., 1902), plate 256.*

General Plan
for the
Improvement
OF THE
U. S. CAPITOL GROUNDS.

FRED. LAW OLMSTED
Landscape Architect

Smithsonian, and the Pension Building in the Judiciary Square area. Meigs's red buildings and Supervising Architect James J. Hill's Bureau of Printing and Engraving on Fourteenth Street broke, if only temporarily, from the classical-styled white public architecture and served as an indication of governmental indecision about official architecture as well as about future sites for public buildings in Washington.

The granite-towered Post Office (figure 14), completed by the century's end, and the green-domed Library of Congress contributed additions to the city's varied skyline. Frederick Law Olmsted provided the recently extended Capitol with a new landscaped platform and western terrace (figure 11). Olmsted's views on a unified Mall echoed the visions of Michler and Babcock.

The years following the Civil War also saw an exceptional burst of municipal activity. Municipal bankruptcy resulting from the excesses of the territorial government did not crush the desire to advance; water, sewer mains, and programs of public works of all sorts were continued with vigor. So, too, were the growth of gas, electric, telephone, transit, and other utility services. But the most significant business activity of the period was undoubtedly real estate with its accompanying work of subdivisions and construction. As new communities grew, so did their articulate civic associations. These needs—and voices—were faithfully reflected in the growing institutions of the press, and became focused in demands for home rule.

The works of private and municipal designers also contributed to the Victorian city. German-born Adolph Cluss designed many of the city's schools and churches, accommodating the growing and flourishing residential population. Cluss also designed many of Dupont Circle's luxurious residences, attracting the affluent, the politically powerful, and the diplomatic corps—and further reinforcing the social divisions of the city. At the turn of the century, Senator Francis Newlands took residential development beyond the city's old boundaries, along Connecticut Avenue into Maryland, in the creation of the new suburban community of Chevy Chase. Many other residential settlements along major streetcar and railroad arteries were also created in the postwar era. Mount Pleasant, Brookland, and Le Droit Park in the county of Washington (beyond the municipal corporate limits but within the District of Columbia) initially were isolated, countrylike, and distinctive neighborhoods, even bounded by fences, but their convenience to the original settlement foreshadowed their ultimate loss of individual identity as they would merge with other settlements in the twentieth century.

The developments on unplatted lands often conformed only to the original

FIGURE 12. *"Uncontrolled Growth," 1927. In a map prepared by the National Capital Park and Planning Commission showing growth of the city outside the L'Enfant Plan, the darkened areas indicate settlements in existence prior to the 1893 official highway plan. In the context of twentieth-century preoccupations with controlled and orderly growth, the often haphazard street layouts were viewed with dismay.*

Courtesy National Capital Planning Commission.

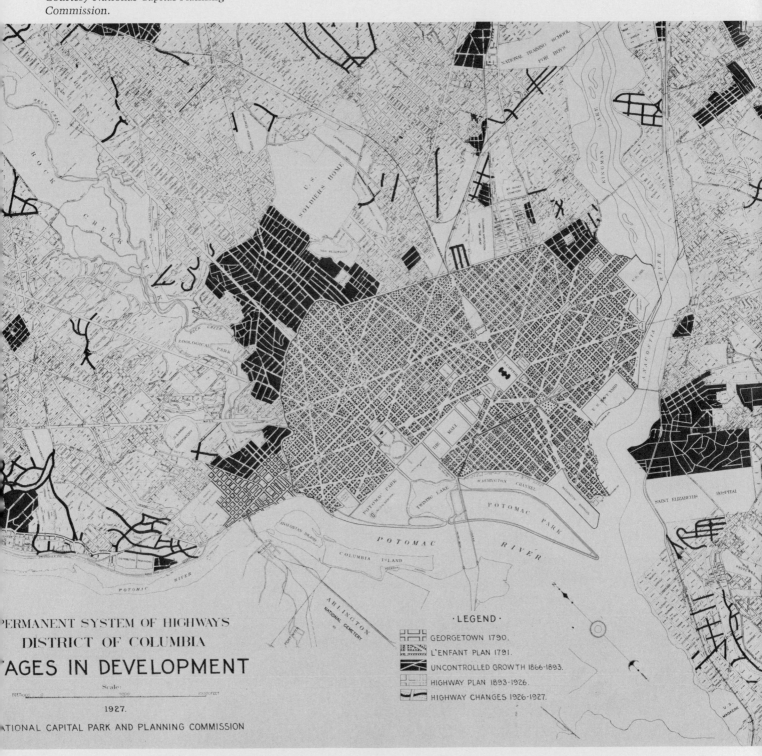

PERMANENT SYSTEM OF HIGHWAYS
DISTRICT OF COLUMBIA
STAGES IN DEVELOPMENT

Scale

FEET 1000   0   1000   10000 FEET

1927.

NATIONAL CAPITAL PARK AND PLANNING COMMISSION

·LEGEND·

GEORGETOWN 1790.

L'ENFANT PLAN 1791.

UNCONTROLLED GROWTH 1866-1893.

HIGHWAY PLAN 1893-1926.

HIGHWAY CHANGES 1926-1927.

opportunistic plans of separate developers. By 1888, the proliferation of independent street systems north of Boundary Street (now Florida Avenue) had created such a discontinuity between the city and the surrounding District that a unified street system was required by the 1888 congressional statute "to regulate the subdivision of land within the District of Columbia." This system of streets was reflected in the rough and ready extension of the radials and grid of the L'Enfant Plan. Little could be done to replat the streets already created by private intentions, however, and even a highway plan drawn in the wake of the stronger 1893 mandate (figure 12) failed to enforce this system of streets on the topographically rugged land closest to Florida Avenue. The new highway system was effective primarily in the then unsettled areas nearest to the District lines.

By the century's end (figures 13, 14), the city's original framework had been filled in and had indeed begun to spill over into the nearby suburban counties. The settlement of the highlands by the affluent left the older

FIGURE 14. *Pennsylvania Avenue a Century Old, ca. 1900. The thoroughfare intended by L'Enfant to exhibit the city's cultural institutions became instead a busy commercial street, lined with office buildings, hotels, and shops. Noteworthy in this view are the Willard Hotel under construction, and the just-completed Post Office Building whose clock tower can be seen in the distance. The agreeable street façades hid from view the sordid slums south of the avenue as well as the fashionable shopping area along F Street .*

Courtesy Washingtoniana Division, Martin Luther King Memorial Library.

basin city to public and commercial interests as well as to the poor and transient population. The provision of services had in effect staked out portions of the city to specific social classes. Although Washington never experienced the urban strife occasioned by vast industrial complexes, it became disturbingly congested. Large crowded areas populated by the poor encouraged the creation of parks intended to relieve the stresses of this congestion, and civic spaces aimed at raising the intellectual consciousness of an urban citizenry were developed according to the doctrines of municipal reform.

1900-1926 The Metropolitan City

The new century opened amid a rousing Centennial celebration of the "removal of the seat of government" to Washington. In the course of intensified discussions surrounding the city's physical future (figure 15), the proposals of many individual architects were recorded in the annual meeting of the American Institute of Architects held that year in the capital city. Their discussions of city improvements ranged from possible groupings of public buildings, parks, statuary, to proposals for the formation of a commission of experts to be responsible for translating the best suggestions into a new plan for the city. Several architects, most notably AIA secretary and historian of the Capitol, Glenn Brown, popularized such issues in the media and at the doors of congressmen. In the following year, these efforts bore fruit in a Senate resolution to study plans for the city's park system. Under the leadership of Senator James McMillan, chairman of the District Committee—but without any concurrent action by the House—a blue ribbon group of urban designers was assembled under the name of the "Senate Park Commission," and given a far-ranging directive that included the designation of sites for public buildings and the design of a comprehensive parks program.

The membership of the McMillan Commission represented the combined talents that had produced the highly influential Chicago 1893 World's Columbian Exposition: architects Daniel H. Burnham and Charles F. McKim, and landscape architect Frederick Law Olmsted, Jr., later joined by sculptor Augustus Saint-Gaudens. Willingly awed by these artistic Olympians, Charles Moore, as secretary to McMillan, served as the commission's executive—and later as its authoritative spokesman and powerful executor. The panel of experts reflected experience in larger and more industrialized cities, New York, Boston, Chicago, cities that had already begun to cope with sheer physical growth on a metropolitan basis. But it also reflected New York taste.

In the work of the commission, its members looked to the American past, to Washington, Jefferson, and L'Enfant, for inspiration. They visited the colonial capitals of Annapolis and Williamsburg. Pushing time back farther, they traveled to Europe's old cities. The Coast and Geodetic Survey provided maps of Washington's topography, and model makers (figures 39, 44) were hired. The final plan, published in 1902 (figure 16), concerned itself with parks in the ceremonial section of the city as well as public buildings, thus expressing the conviction of Burnham and Olmsted that policies for public buildings and for parks were inextricably intertwined. The plan's regional perspective, from Mount Vernon to Great Falls, was a notable advance over nineteenth-century preoccupation with the city proper.

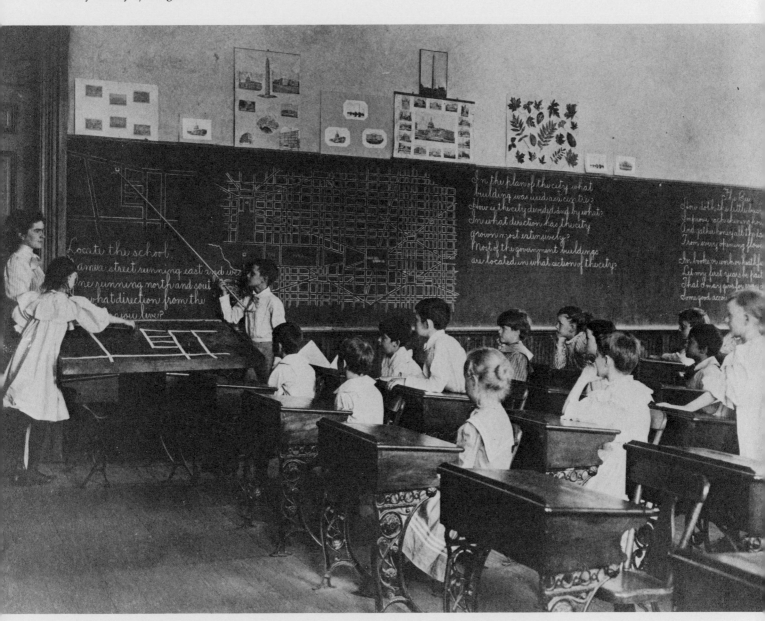

Had L'Enfant seen and read the plan, he would hardly have recognized his own contributions. The city had greatly increased in extent. The land covered by the McMillan Plan included all of the additions and extensions provided by reclamation of the flats. The addition of land to the west of the Washington Monument was dedicated to a memorial to President Lincoln, the two memorials symbolically linked by a decorative canal (later the Reflecting Pool) recalling the ancient but buried waters of Tiber Creek. The

33

FIGURE 16. *The McMillan Commission Plan for the Mall, 1901–1902. The McMillan Commission sought to reestablish the formal outlines of the city as reinterpreted from L'Enfant's original intentions. Here the Mall is given strict linear configurations. Passing through the Washington Monument area, the Mall is joined to the Lincoln Memorial on the reclaimed flats by a long decorative canal shown here with a north-south segment. (The present Reflecting Pool carries out the canal concept.) The railroad station,* *formerly located on the Mall, was removed to an area northeast of the Capitol. The shorter cross axis is given greater dimension in this plan by the proposed siting of a national pantheon adjacent to the newly formed Tidal Basin.*
Courtesy National Capital Planning Commission.

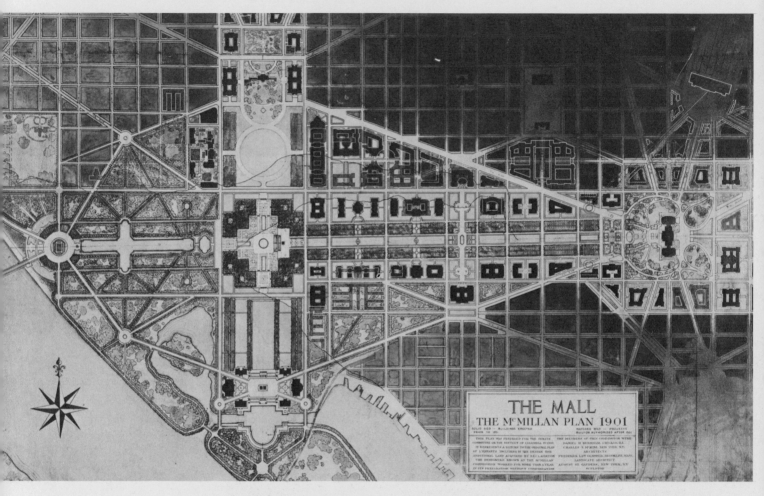

THE MALL
THE McMILLAN PLAN 1901

mile-long axis of the Mall now extended from the Capitol to the Washington Monument, and across the projected Arlington Memorial Bridge, ending up in the Virginia hills at Arlington House. To the north of the canal, the commission suggested a wood, similar to Paris's Bois de Boulogne. The new lands created to the south of the Mall were to be recreational spaces, with another spot appropriate for a memorial at the conjunction of the White House axis with Maryland Avenue, perhaps a pantheon to the authors of the Constitution.

The Mall (figure 17) was re-established in its formality, unified and stripped of the Downing-inspired undulating walks as well as the intrusive railroad station and tracks, long a civic disfigurement. Elms were to be planted along the Mall's longitudinal edges (figure 42), defining this space and its central panel of sward. The Washington Monument, unhappily irrevocably located

FIGURE 17. *Rendering of the McMillan Commission Plan for the Mall, 1901–1902. The resculpted grounds of the Washington Monument joined the L'Enfant monumental center with the extensions of land to the west and south reclaimed in the late nineteenth century by the Army Corps of Engineers. The circular pond fronting the monument established, as if by illusion, the true central point of the White House–Washington Monument axis. Here the Mall is lined with straight rows of trees and monumental pub-* *lic buildings. B Street (later called Constitution Avenue) is part of this new formality, bordering both the north side of the Mall and the south side of the triangular piece of land which echoes the public purposes of the Mall.*
Courtesy Library of Congress.

off the intended White House–Monument axis because of the uncertainties about its foundations, was to be surrounded by a sunken garden with a great round pool constructed to "realign" the two structures along the true axis. New executive office buildings were to be grouped around Lafayette Square facing the White House. The area south of Pennsylvania Avenue was viewed as potentially a distinctive section of the city, possibly a site for District government buildings. Clearly the McMillan Plan, for all its genuflections to the past, was not the asserted revival of L'Enfant intentions. It was a new plan stretched over an expanded and much altered topography. The frequent references to L'Enfant were made more in the spirit of historical justification rather than as citing models for a twentieth-century plan.

The McMillan Plan might have emphasized primarily ceremonial aspects had the experience and sympathies of the younger Olmsted not been present.

Reflecting the experience of his colleague, Charles Eliot, and the Boston metropolitan park system, Olmsted contributed suggestions as to how Washington's parks might be connected and developed along attractive drives. A single comprehensive and unified park system was necessary, including an improved Rock Creek Park and the reclamation of the Anacostia flats which now reduplicated the unhealthy conditions of the Potomac flats of only two decades earlier. Although much of the Rock Creek Valley was in public ownership, it was described as "shabby, sordid, and disagreeable," and required a formal treatment with drives and carefully planted rows of trees. The Anacostia flats needed to be dredged, reclaimed, dammed, and walled, both to deal with the problem of sedimentation and in order that a more formal embankment be created. A quay treatment was suggested along the Potomac River connecting Potomac Park and the Pennsylvania Avenue Bridge. A Mount Vernon Parkway—as earlier surveyed by Peter Hains—connecting Washington's home with the city was also proposed. The Civil War system of circumferential fortifications (figure 8), still largely in public ownership and strategically situated to command sweeping panoramic views of the central city, were to be joined in a Fort Drive.

In Olmsted's view, parks were more than places for promenading and repose. They were an integral part of a humanized city, tied to the planning process, and therefore necessarily a part of a functional program to acquire land. With the joining of parks and planning, parks became more democratic, serving the popular needs in recreational purposes: playing fields, bathing beaches, and provisions for boating. Olmsted suggested that over a thousand acres of land and river space along the Anacostia be acquired in order to limit impending heavy industrial development that would cut off access from the eastern sections of the city to large recreational grounds. Parks outside of the ceremonial core were to be developed as neighborhood parks, subject to intensive use, rather than as the havens of leisurely quiet as provided by the Victorian landscape gardeners.

The response of Congress was not immediate. No formal implementation of the McMillan Plan was provided except as individual building projects won approval. Nor was support for the various proposals unanimous in the local community. While pleased that the McMillan Commission recommendations appeared to have abated the threat that Congress would give the Pennsylvania Railroad a large part of the Mall, the city was troubled by the financial implications of the plan; fears of its excessive formalism were still being voiced as late as 1910. The fact that the issue surfaced in newspaper cartoons (figure 43) illustrated its current vitality and ability to arouse public

FIGURE 18. *Union Station and the City Post Office, 1920. The construction of Union Station northeast of the Capitol (1903–1907) signaled a major triumph of the McMillan Commission's plans for the monumental core. Daniel H. Burnham designed the station, called the "vestibule" to the nation's capital. This structure was complemented in 1914 by the similarly styled City Post Office just to the west (on North Capitol Street).*

Courtesy Library of Congress.

interest. Actually, early success in removing obstacles to the fulfillment of the plan depended more on individual negotiations—on specific projects—between members of the commission and those empowered with decision making. For example, Daniel Burnham persuaded Pennsylvania Railroad President Alexander Cassatt to remove the railroad station and tracks from the Mall to a site to the north, now Union Station (figure 18). Pressure was also applied to retain the new Department of Agriculture Building along the

37

building lines outlined by the plan, in the grove of trees rather than projecting into the intended green panel of the Mall.

The success of the McMillan Plan was to be measured not in immediate congressional actions but in its long-term influence on public parks and building in the city. Strongest support for the plan came from the president and the Washington business community. Just as the Chicago World's Fair dominated architectural styles for half a century, so the powerful images created by the McMillan Plan served as a model for Washington designers for many decades and exemplified the best in the classical revival. The plan stood forth as an inspiring set piece of the City Beautiful movement that was to sweep the nation.

One major aid in casting a long memory of the architectural qualities of the 1902 plan was the Commission of Fine Arts, created in 1910. Responsible initially for advising on public sculptures in the capital city, the commission had its mandate extended soon after to public buildings as well. Burnham and Olmsted served on this commission, with the McMillan Plan further embodied in Charles Moore, long-time chairman of the commission and powerful arbiter of taste through to the 1930s. At long last, federal commitment to the city was at hand, both in this commission and in its presidential endorsements.

World War I brought on a significant pause in the work of civic improvement. Moreover, construction of temporary office buildings (often concrete and destined to last in some cases for fifty years) and housing for government war workers filled important areas, such as that between the Capitol and Union Station, and added new problems. Most of all, the war swelled the city's population to permanently higher levels, exacerbating all other problems of physical growth and expansion.

In the early 1920s, in spite of these many difficulties, the work of capital building resumed in earnest. During the following decades, major recommendations of the McMillan Commission would be fulfilled: the Lincoln Memorial and the Reflecting Pool were constructed, the Memorial Bridge was completed, and grand, classical institutional and public structures were built along the Mall and north up Seventeenth Street and at Lafayette Square. Notable among these structures are the Pan American Union Building, Constitution Hall, and the Department of Agriculture Building. Cass Gilbert's Treasury Annex, standing as the only realized portion of an executive building enclave intended to surround Lafayette Square, was given architectural companionship in the mid-1920s by the Gilbert-designed Chamber of Commerce Building.

In other parts of the city significant urban design problems were to be faced and resolved. Surrounding Union Station, additional buildings, related commercial structures, and a large landscape design problem appeared. The foot of Capitol Hill, where the Olmstedian informality of the Capitol grounds joined the geometric formality of the Mall, was another question mark. And around the Capitol Square the growth of the legislative establishment required a major group of new monumental buildings; Capitol Hill itself was emerging as an important concentration of libraries, museums, and cultural institutions. The Commission of Fine Arts had a full agenda.

The ultimate accolade for Charles Moore, commission chairman, came from the revered architect William Adams Delano in an intimate memoir written for the Century Association, the New York club that had been the scene of so many planning endeavors. After citing Cass Gilbert, Henry Bacon, Paul Philippe Cret, and John Russell Pope as the architects who had stamped the character of modern Washington, Delano wrote, ". . . if one had to name the man most responsible for the development of our present capital it would be Charles Moore."

The expanding city that was to receive the new ceremonial core and parks system was meanwhile filling the District's boundaries and spilling over. The emerging metropolitan city had developed along streetcar and railroad lines radiating out from the ceremonial core of the city into the rest of the District, Maryland, and Virginia, and had produced chains of commuting towns that sprouted around railroad stations and depots. As the parallel highway system developed, business districts then formed along these strips. The cost of land also increased, necessitating the most productive use of resources possible. To the north of well-planned and often luxurious mansions and townhouses, block upon block of modest row houses were developed, single-family dwellings of distinctly urban character without pretensions to countrylike or even suburban amenities. Outside the District's boundaries, residents were now offered the presumed benefits of small town and rural lifestyles. This system of settlements radiating from a central core—no matter that congestion increased along the routes—was considered an ideal urban arrangement by contemporary humanists. Major open spaces separated the "spokes of the wheel" was the rationale, open spaces that were not convenient to mass commuter traffic but were accessible to the adjoining neighborhoods.

The automobile drastically altered this neat configuration. By 1925, this mode of transportation seemed to be irreversibly accepted by the nation. No longer did residential settlements need to be near the streetcar or railroad station. Residential areas could be diffused, built anywhere a road led, and soon serviced by business clusters equally free of rail constraints. The process of decentralization of the city, the creation of suburbs having already commenced with the rail system, was thus given greater impetus by the automobile. The outlines of the city were transformed under a less visually manageable sprawling pattern of urbanization. Just as business districts followed the residential dispersal in the form of shopping centers, employment centers later dispersed as well. It was no longer necessary for one to travel to the old core of the city in order to find work.

The dimensions of the city as well as its definitive configuration were dramatically affected by the automobile. Whereas neighborhoods (figure 63) had been conceived as unique and well-defined lineal entities, along streetcar routes, the auto enabled new residential strips to join old enclaves, breaking down the physical and social isolation and populating all available spaces in the street system established in the late 1890s by the highway commission. The McMillan Commission had pointed to the failure to acquire parkland in these areas. In filling the volume of the District's ten-mile square, the future of the city lay not in annexing and consolidating new spaces as other American cities would, but in implementing the realization that Washington was a metropolitan city. Planning for parks and further development would have to be met in an intergovernmental structure.

Zoning and planning agencies had already taken root in cities. Embryonic public planning in Washington in the modern period can be traced at least to the 1890s' street-highway plan, the 1899 curb on heights of buildings, and more explicitly the 1920 zoning of land use supplied by planner Harland Bartholomew—virtually a continuous if not yet institutionalized planning process. In the expanding suburbs the pressure for planning was exhibited in the activities of the Washington Suburban Sanitary Commission. The progressive business and civic committees in the city argued for more regulatory powers (especially in the interest of real estate values), despite the protests of Charles Moore that the Commission of Fine Arts and its interpretations of the 1902 McMillan Plan constituted all that was needed for Washington planning.

In 1924, Congress created the National Capital Park Commission in order to implement the park provisions as originally suggested in the nineteenth century and as summarized and extended by the McMillan Commission. Providing further continuity with the past, the Park Commission's membership included the Corps of Engineers as well as other ex officio representatives. Park acquisitions were important, but they were additionally significant in the siting of urban functions such as transportation, housing, recrea-

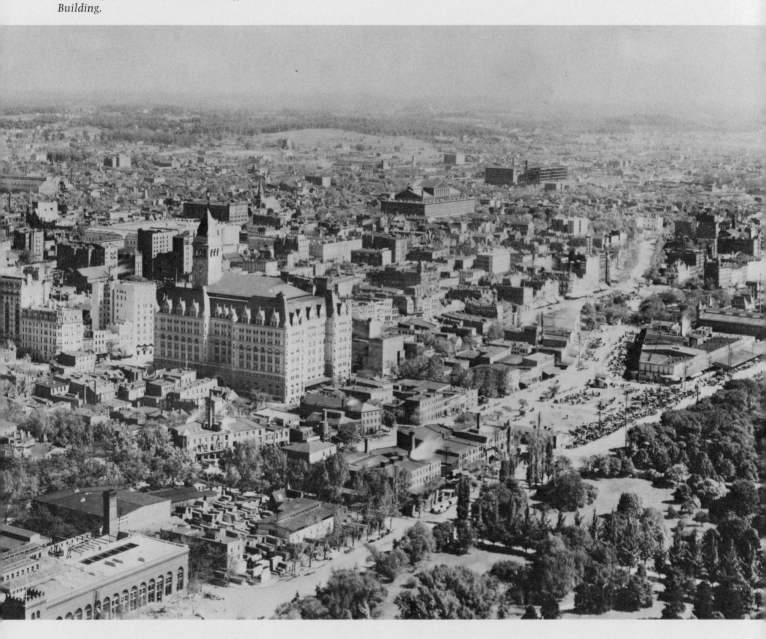

tion, and public buildings. Modern city planning was everywhere coming into being, reflecting this relationship.

Thus, two years later, in 1926, a public law was enacted replacing the Park Commission with the National Capital Park and Planning Commission (NCPPC). Frederick Law Olmsted, Jr., the leading figure in his profession whose authority was reinforced by his service on the McMillan Commission

FIGURE 20. *Suggested Architectural Treatment for the Federal Triangle, 1926. The separate monumental buildings of the Federal Triangle were designed by various prominent architectural firms but harmonized by the coordination of the over-all design for landscaping and statuary by Edward Bennett, coordinating architect for the Federal Triangle and advisor to Secretary of the Treasury Andrew Mellon.*

Theodore Horydczak photograph, courtesy National Capital Planning Commission.

as well as later work, was appointed by the president to serve on the NCPPC. His experience was complemented by that of Frederic Delano, an important figure in the creation of the 1908 Chicago plan and the 1929 New York Regional Plan; Jesse C. Nichols, a nationally celebrated real estate developer and creator of the country club district of Kansas City, Missouri; and Milton Medary, president of the American Institute of Architects. In gaining specific and significant planning powers, the commission was instructed to coordinate plans and perform studies in conjunction with similar agencies set up in Maryland and Virginia; to carry on city planning in the District; to absorb the duties of the Highway Commission, a significant operating program; and to purchase properties for parks, parkways, and playgrounds. This initial view of the new function of government assumed that there would be coordination, leadership, and a response to the unified vision of the city's future, but did not recognize this would have to be given detailed expression and force by a new agency.

While the metropolitan city was acknowledged in the creation of the National Capital Park and Planning Commission, the monumental core was also about to be provided with an unprecedented stamp of grandeur. In the early years of the century, much congressional and public attention was focused on the supervising architect's office, especially as increasing governmental services required new public building in both Washington and the rest of the country. The Public Building Act of 1913 had instructed the Public Buildings Commission to devise standards for public buildings. While the commission and its various successor bodies made annual reports on the subject, little was done to accommodate the expanded civil service ranks crowded in Washington's rented space in private buildings. Finally, in 1926, in the face of headlines exposing the government's "million dollar rent bill," the new Public Building Act appropriated $50 million to construct public buildings in the District. The planning body provided in the act outlined twelve buildings to be constructed in the triangular space formed by L'Enfant's two major axes and bounded by Pennsylvania Avenue, Constitution Avenue, and Fourteenth Street, the Federal Triangle (figures 19, 20). In this large seventy-acre tract of land, monumental structures of an eclectic but over-all harmonious design were to be constructed during the next decade, to present to the public a symbol of the power of the national government.

In the creation of the Federal Triangle, the business district around the Center Market—whose deterioration had accelerated during the Civil War—was to be replaced by the unified grouping of monumental government buildings. Swamppoodle, Murder Bay, and other notorious slum communities had to go. This renewal–large scale planning relationship would take place in the static yet evolving city planned by L'Enfant.

The Federal Triangle was developed as a group of buildings complete in itself (figure 53), but it was hardly an example of good planning. It lacked any real context in the comprehensive plan for the city as a whole; there was no integrated reason for its location here. No anticipation of the needs of such a concentration of federal office workers had embraced the practical details of how they got to work, where they had lunch, or where they parked their cars. It was a toss-up whether Secretary of the Treasury Andrew Mellon would recommend the federal development of both sides of Pennsylvania Avenue—or whether to expect a vigorous private response of developers on the north side of the avenue in the form of new hotels, stores, theaters, and other buildings. Neither alternative eventuated. The newly created National Capital Park and Planning Commission was almost immediately drawn into efforts to deal with these questions, and even with details of the Federal

Triangle design as its coordinating architect Edward Bennett (figure 20) had proposed them. Fifty years later successive presidential commissions would be wrestling with the problems of "completing" the Federal Triangle, redesigning Pennsylvania Avenue, and even the rudimentary need for removing a thousand parked cars from the Grand Plaza that was to have functioned as the largest central design feature of the Triangle.

The year 1926 marked a decisive turning point in Washington planning. Until then those federal agencies that had earlier located in the District away from the central core (e.g., the Bureau of Standards and the Soldiers' Home, figure 64) had done so for environmental reasons. Now, the mobility offered by the automobile and the rapid communication provided by the telephone enabled public buildings to be located in the far reaches of the District and out into the surrounding counties. These new centers of employment attracted residential and commercial development, urbanizing once-rural counties. Because the District would persist in being defined by its historic ten-mile square, its metropolitan functioning would be increasingly dependent on coordinating planning decisions with surrounding jurisdictions. For this reason and also because it was continually subject to change, strengthening, renewal, and replanning, the city was dealt with in fact on a metropolitan basis.

1926-1960 The Regional City

To meet new urban tasks of metropolitan scope, new planning arrangements were needed. For the past fifty years, Washington regional planners had faced managing the simultaneous transformation of the traditional configurations of the downtown section as well as the radiating peripheral residential settlements. Planning now evolved from the generalized tasks filled by architects, engineers, and "planners" into the specialized planning functions. Urban planning had to become more than physical planning. It became social, economic, and governmental as well. The initial concerns of planners—parks and public buildings—became only two elements of the complex urban network now to encompass regional highways, mass transit, unparalleled population and economic growth, dispersal of functions at an unprecedented scale, and the creation of new modes of human settlement. The city adjusted itself to several emergencies: the depression, the war, and, in the atomic age, the fear of concentrating all governmental buildings in the vulnerable core. There was further impetus to the dispersal of government agencies. The L'Enfant city, once the scope for the entire capital, became the core of a vast metropolitan region. The outlines of the original plan remained a historical artifact to be reinterpreted in terms of the city's present role as the dominant employment and activity center in the region.

A regional transportation and park system were elements of the National Capital Park and Planning Commission's early work. The members and staff also studied the port, industrial and commercial needs, housing, the effects of the automobile on physical growth, and the maintenance and enhancement of the area's rich topographical features. Among the early recommendations of the commission, a weblike configuration of urban highways was drawn up, with major radials linked by circumferential roads. A new regional park system emerged combining the elements of the earlier proposed Fort Drive, parks along the edges of the Potomac and Anacostia Rivers, the extension of Rock Creek Park into Maryland, and neighborhood recreation centers.

Despite its meager staff resources, but with substantial aid from cooperating federal agencies, the new planning commission forged ahead and between 1926 and 1929 formulated the elements of a comprehensive plan that was displayed with much fanfare. An impressive integration of many earlier proposals, this authoritative look into the future provided a document that aroused broad community support.

The initial work of the National Capital Park and Planning Commission (NCPPC) was immediately followed by supportive developments. In 1927, the Maryland–National Capital Park and Planning Commission (M-NCPPC) had been established as a multijurisdictional body. Like the federal commission, it too reflected the regional city created by the automobile, the need for planning for highways and recreation, and the need for zoning subdivision controls, building codes, and other regulatory powers. Much of the suburban Maryland commission's early work was focused on carrying out the guidelines set by the NCPPC in Montgomery and Prince Georges Counties, especially in highways and park proposals.

The 1928 regional park system developed by the NCPPC was facilitated by the 1930 Capper-Cramton Act, which provided funds for the George Washington Memorial Parkway and the Anacostia parks system. The George Washington Parkway was an extension of the Mount Vernon Parkway recommended by Olmsted in the 1902 plan, which traced a pleasure drive from Washington to Mount Vernon. The proposed parkway as seen in 1930 ran from Great Falls to Mount Vernon on the Virginia side of the Potomac and was mirrored on the Maryland side by a parkway from Fort Washington north again to Great Falls. With this vast regional highway, linking two states and the District of Columbia, much of the Potomac River's edges was

FIGURE 21. *New City Housing, 1942. The Frederick Douglass Housing Project, constructed by the National Capital Housing Authority, reflected the philosophies of its director, John Ihlder. Low-rise single-family housing units were constructed in variations of twins and rows. While humane in comparison to later high-rise public housing, the Douglass project because of its location in the distant Anacostia area raised strong criticism. Lack of public transportation to employment or access to other city services were severe disadvantages of this location. Courtesy Library of Congress.*

defined by park strips, offering appropriately ceremonial approaches to the city. New bridges over the Potomac and the Anacostia provided essential links in the railroad system. The Capper-Cramton Act also provided for the protection of Rock Creek and its branches, as well as for the extension of parks along the Anacostia River and its stream valleys into Maryland. The protection of Virginia's stream valleys was also outlined, but was never developed as extensively as on the opposite shore because of the inability of the northern Virginia jurisdictions to raise their share of the funds.

The demands of the depression and World War II found in the NCPPC's plans a fertile source of public works projects—but also set the stage for testing the commission's powers. In some cases, other decision-making agencies invaded the work of the commission. As housing and new social concerns dominated the physical growth of the city (figure 21), agencies such as the Housing Division of the Public Works Administration made important independent planning decisions. The location of major federal installations—especially the Pentagon—across the river in Virginia reflected the lack of official support for the work of the NCPPC, which had intended such build-

FIGURE 22. *Post–World War II View of the Monumental Core. The Mall reflected the aspirations of the McMillan Commission but was still marred by blocks of wartime "tempos." Implementation of planning policy, however, would soon create major changes not reflected in this photograph. The Federal Triangle to the north (upper right of picture) of the Mall is largely completed in this view, although the full completion of the design was compromised by the supremacy of the automobile and changing attitudes* *toward classical monumentalism.*

Courtesy Fairchild Aerial Surveys, Inc.

47

ings to be located in the city's monumental core. Moreover, the NCPPC had
envisioned the land on which the Pentagon is located as being reserved for
park purposes. Not only was parkland lost in the construction of the Pentagon, but as Department of Interior Secretary Harold Ickes summarized, the
building, a virtual city in itself, created "upsetting influences involving
shifting population, traffic congestion, and a general disturbance of the
whole city pattern." Important new roads were planned by the commission,

FIGURE 24. *Suburban Sprawl Centering around Historic Rockville, ca. 1954. The agricultural lands surrounding the nineteenth-century railroad suburb of Rockville in Montgomery County were giving way to the curved-street developments of the postwar suburban boom. Actually focused on the highway, this growth often seemed haphazard and its apparent formlessness inspired concern for direction and control.*
Courtesy Fairchild Aerial Services, Inc.

and built, to Fort Meade and other installations. The wartime needs of the military were met in constructing throughout the District's parklands temporary office space and housing, sited to facilitate their later removal (figure 22).

Any expectation, however, of returning the post–World War II city to its prewar status was shattered by the further dispersal of federal agencies throughout the region, partly in response to the fear of concentrating highly sensitive bureaus all within range of possible atomic bomb attack, and partly because the central city could not physically accommodate all federal employment. Examples of this dispersal on the Maryland side included the Atomic Energy Commission in Germantown, the Bureau of Standards at Gaithersburg, and the National Security Agency at Fort Meade. But dispersal was also fed by other motivations, such as the search for more efficient types of office buildings and for the green, campuslike environment demanded by many federal installations. The physical facilitators of dispersal—the belt roads and extended radials—were recommended in the NCPPC's 1950 Comprehensive Plan for the National Capital and Its Environs.

While this 1950 plan reflected the physical dispersal of the city into the vast suburban region (figures 23, 24), it recognized the accompanying expansion of the central employment area and the larger network of facilities this would demand. The continuing concern with the evolving central area within a regional context is indication that the plan was drawn up initially to serve as a basis for the redevelopment of "obsolete neighborhoods" in the District. The 1945 District of Columbia Redevelopment Act had directed the Planning Commission to produce such a plan. In its most dramatic section, expressing the new emphasis on housing and redevelopment, the 1950 plan inventoried dwellings throughout the District, delineating areas of overcrowding, primitive sanitation facilities, delinquency, disease, and inadequate neighborhood facilities. In the attention given inner city neighborhoods, the plan represented a shift from the federal emphasis of the Planning Commission to a greater concern with the constituent city, but important planning proposals included the East Mall, the Northwest Rectangle, and the Southwest Rectangle. The plan also reflected historical roots as it looked back to the beginning years of the NCPPC and its early park proposals, which themselves had taken inspiration from the L'Enfant and McMillan plans.

Despite the issuance in 1950 of the long-awaited plan, the circumstances of the preceding decade and a half produced growing arguments for a reorganized Planning Commission. The park acquisition function as defined by the Capper-Cramton Act had served as an important physical product of

FIGURE 25. *The Effects of the Capital Beltway on the Landscape, 1968. The predominance of the automobile has allowed for the carving of formerly agricultural lands into far-flung suburban settlements. No longer entirely dependent on the central city for employment and shopping, these settlements embrace their own office buildings, shopping centers, recreational grounds, and residential clusters. The dispersal process has been abetted by the decentralization of govern-ment facilities into the far reaches of the regional city.*

Courtesy Virginia Department of Highways and U.S. Bureau of Public Roads.

the Planning Commission's work. By the late 1950s, however, this acquisition program had been largely completed. It was clear that planning entailed more of the urban aspects of the city, especially highways, housing, commercial and industrial clusters, employment centers, and educational facilities.

In recognizing the fulfillment of the 1930 federal program for parks, an act of 1952 redefined the Planning Commission as the National Capital Planning Commission (NCPC), deleting the reference to parks and adding members reflecting the intensified urban concerns: the ex officio commissioner of public roads, and two of five presidential appointees qualified by their residence in the District. The NCPC was directed to concentrate its planning efforts in the District and on federal activities in the region. Nonfederal regional issues, largely concerning highways and dispersal, were to be coordinated by a newly created National Capital Regional Planning Council (NCRPC).

In the upsurge of concern with population mobility—both the daily commuting and the longer-term migration from the District into the suburban counties—highway planning and dispersal occupied the attention of planners in the 1950s. The decisive new feature was the 75-mile Capital Beltway which would begin to be used in 1968 (figure 25). Proposed by both the NCPC and the NCRPC and constructed at an average distance of twelve miles from the urban center, this urban expressway—part of the Federal Interstate System launched in 1956—"filled in" the radial spokes of the idealized Victorian and early twentieth century city. Along this new circumferential expressway, at interchanges with main radial routes, major business, commercial, and educational centers developed. Visual and spatial references were now made in terms of whether new development occurred inside or outside the Beltway, and at distances and directions from its interchanges. In the linkage of the Maryland and Virginia suburbs, the Beltway formed a new boundary which itself serves as the core—much in the same way as the original L'Enfant city did and later the District's ten-mile square—of a vaster regional city. And as this Beltway core began to be filled in, studies would be made considering outer beltways.

Despite the new platforms for mobility, the days of the population's exclusive preoccupation with highways were numbered. In 1955, a congressional appropriation was made to both the NCPC and the Regional Planning Council to conduct a survey of present and future transit needs. In 1959, the two agencies reported, from their studies of land use and projected developments, that if highways continued to be the dominant mode of transportation, monstrous new expressways with capacities ranging from four to twenty-six lanes would need to be built. Faced with such a specter of urban devastation, the agencies recommended a coordinated system as well as improvements to existing highways. Out of this report, the National Capital Transportation Agency was created to plan and develop what is now the Metro rapid transit system.

Closely harnessed to the 1950 Comprehensive Plan effort was a zoning study (undertaken in 1955 by the consultant Harold M. Lewis) of the often-amended act of 1 March 1920 creating the District Zoning Commission. Antedating the establishment of any planning agency—and providing a built-in point of conflict—the zoning act had been implemented by the District commissioners with the assistance of staff provided by the engineer commissioner's office. Earlier regulation of building height and the preclusion of business from residential districts were part of the nineteenth-century planning history of the city, but the 1920 act was among the earliest in the nation to authorize the division of the city into districts "within which the height, use and area of buildings to be erected" was regulated. Both by act of Congress and in a growing body of cases flowing from judicial review of the ordinance, zoning powers were considerably amplified. With the 1926 planning act, Congress had specified the "orderly development as the National Capital" among the purposes of zoning, and required that zoning regulations be made in accordance with a comprehensive plan. This use of zoning as a tool of comprehensive planning motivated the 1955 review of zoning. It was hoped that Lewis's work would eliminate or at least moderate the numerous conflicts between the Board of Zoning Adjustment and the Planning Commission.

The evolution of zoning in Washington was not markedly different from the experience of other cities, Lewis found, but in viewing Washington as a capital city he was able to identify certain special provisions. Outstanding among these were architectural controls to ensure that the development of the city, in the language of Congress, "should proceed along the lines of good order, good taste, and with due regard to the public interests involved." Among the special, regulated areas so defined were areas abutting on the Capitol, the White House, and other public buildings and parks. A similar regulatory provision was later applied to protect Georgetown as a historic district.

Following Lewis's recommendations, the 1950 Comprehensive Plan as subsequently revised by the Planning Commission staff was taken as the basis for further considerations. Among the most important of the new considerations was that relating to the development of neighborhood land use plans.

For this purpose the city was divided into 137 neighborhoods. Each neighborhood was bounded by major transportation routes—called into being by modern automobile traffic—or by parks or institutional buffering lands. Each neighborhood, furthermore, had sufficient population to support one public elementary school. This recognition of the significance of the automobile in urban design, and the influence of Clarence Arthur Perry's study of the neighborhood unit in the 1929 New York Regional Plan, saw Washington's planning responding more to nationwide influences than to its own past history of concern with the neighborhood unit, although in practice the difference was not great. Moreover, in the words of the Lewis report, "the city is largely developed and zoning cannot be expected to alter drastically the general pattern of existing land uses." In the map describing the neighborhoods identified in the Lewis report, the central core of the city was shown virtually surrounded by about forty so-called "problem neighborhoods" south and east of the Capitol and north of Massachusetts Avenue. In these neighborhoods, Lewis thought, public action would be required to overcome deficiencies in residential conditions, school or recreational facilities, and off-street parking, or to meet other specific needs. Following the 1950 plan, he warned that these conditions had been brought to light for the first time in his analysis, and reported that "other areas not so shown are experiencing difficulty of a lesser degree of criticalness" and were "in danger of becoming problem areas if not carefully developed or redeveloped." This was a finding highly compatible with the urban redevelopment philosophy of the times, and was soon translated into the Shaw, Northwest, Northeast, and H Street redevelopment areas, as well as into the massive private conversion and restoration of the Capitol Hill residential district.

1961-1976 The Continuing Plan

In 1961, the National Capital Planning Commission and the National Capital Regional Planning Council issued "A Policies Plan for the Year 2000." Just as the L'Enfant Plan was accepted by the McMillan Commission as the basis for its work, and these two historic planning efforts together constituted the beginnings of the comprehensive planning work of the National Capital Park and Planning Commission in 1926, so the 1961 plan both continued the earlier work of more than a century and a half but also introduced important new initiatives (figure 26). In the growth of the metropolitan region, the changes in function and design of the central city, and the new planning powers and changing interpretations of the federal and local interest, the Policies Plan found many new options. Notable also is its exceptionally long

FIGURE 26. *Outlines of the Year 2000 Plan, 1961. In this diagrammatic view, the large central circle represents the Metro-Center, while the long radials, containing highways and rapid rail, connect major subcenters of either new towns or old suburban settlements. Washington is clearly defined here as a vast regional city. The darkened areas between the spokes represent wedges of parklands and other open space as well as land devoted to low-density use.*

Courtesy National Capital Planning Commission.

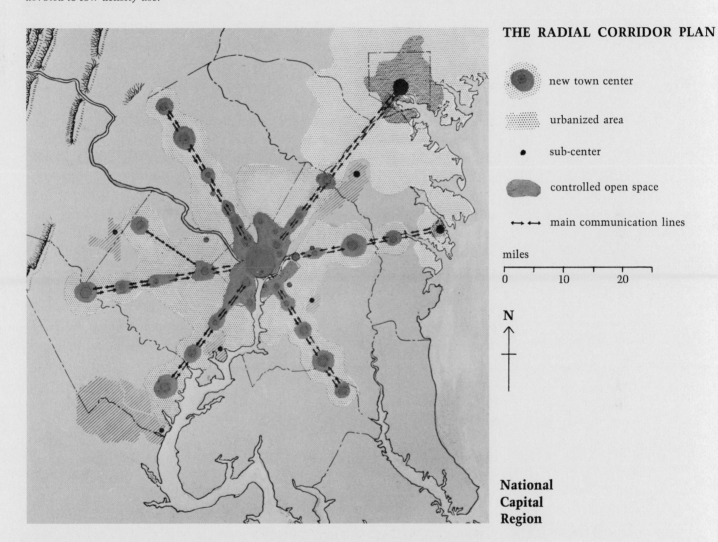

THE RADIAL CORRIDOR PLAN

new town center

urbanized area

sub-center

controlled open space

↔ ↔ main communication lines

miles

0	10	20

N

National Capital Region

span of anticipation—forty years, or nearly twice the conventional future time of most comprehensive city plans. Sometimes described as a "kite-flying exercise," the Policies Plan did offer many tentative ideas. These were nonetheless seriously entertained and succeeded in arousing widespread public discussion throughout the region and in high federal circles. The feedback from community consideration of the 1961 plan occasioned more detailed studies within the NCPC and NCRPC staffs and in the discussions of the commission. Many of these studies were summarized in the 1965 report of the commission (the so-called "Brown Book") and the 1966 Regional Development Guide of the council.

Differing from the L'Enfant and McMillan plans, the 1961 plan was of comparable dramatic value. Growth was cited as the most important single factor in the region's development and future prospects. The task of the NCPC was, therefore, to direct growth so that new urban and suburban communities would be developed in an orderly fashion, retaining the aesthetic and recreational amenities of the open countryside. The plan offered alternatives. The recommended configuration drawn up to encompass these two major objectives was described as the "radial corridor plan" (also known as "wedges and corridors"). Superficially it was similar, although on a much magnified scale, to the old streetcar pattern with major transportation and settlement areas occurring in radial lines emanating from the central core. Believing that a mass transit system, a modern, rationalized version of the once-thriving system of streetcars and railroads, would meet twentieth-century needs, the Year 2000 Plan foresaw the orderly growth of the city occurring in planned secondary town centers developed along these radials, a pattern to be achieved by the strategic location of federal employment. Such "new town" capabilities were just emerging as in the plan for Reston, Virginia. Freeways would be planned to reinforce the new patterns created by mass transit. The routes of the transportation system allowed for easy access to the central city; at the same time, the communities along its right of way could sustain independent employment, commercial, and residential functions as far away as forty miles from the center. In the wedges between the urbanized radials, vast open spaces totaling 300,000 acres would be preserved to ensure the integrity of the plan.

Essential to the realization of the radial development was the construction of the rapid transit system. The modern secondary centers along the corridors were more complex. These were diversified clusters of office buildings, apartment houses, other concentrated residential groupings, a shopping center, a community center, schools, and industry, all surrounded by outlying parks, farms, and forests. The major open spaces to be administered by public agencies were to contain rural characteristics indigenous to the area (dairying in upper Montgomery County and tobacco farming along the Patuxent River in Prince Georges County), as well as low density development, e.g., Dulles Airport at Chantilly, Virginia, and the Agricultural Research Center at Beltsville, Maryland. The green wedges would also preserve the woodlands, stream valleys, and unspoiled wilderness areas and their ecology.

Although the Year 2000 Plan provided for major employment along the densely populated corridors, most of the L'Enfant city and much of the District would continue to be the major employment center, the employers including the federal agencies, local governments, and business, industrial, and institutional establishments. In fact, the attractiveness of the core was due to its variety of functions, strengthened by the plan and physically denoted by a "harmonious mixture of building shapes and styles." The Year 2000 Plan also provided alternative plans for the siting of public buildings—in smaller "cells" placed in the blighted areas and serving both as impetus to renewal and as "visual pauses" along the monumental avenues. Open spaces so crucial to the proposed wedges and corridors would be created in the monumental core as well. The plan designated "special streets" that would connect both existing and expanded parkland in the city to serve as a "constant source of orientation and delight."

In its updating of the 1950 version of the regional city, the Year 2000 Plan won the endorsement of President Kennedy. Although no specific details were provided as to how the plan might be implemented, its "guidebook" to new planning policies made a powerful impression on the long-range planning of the National Capital Planning Commission, the park and planning agencies in the suburban counties, as well as the cosponsoring National Capital Regional Planning Council, forerunner of the planning function of the present Council of Governments (COG).

In Maryland, the wedges and corridors concept was well adapted to the state's historical and contemporary configurations. Major settlements had occurred along what is now Interstate 270 towards Frederick, Maryland; the present Interstate 95 between Washington and Baltimore; and Maryland Route 5 south to Waldorf. Major wedges of green spaces already separated these corridors. On the Virginia side, however, the relative isolation of the area—by nature of the Potomac River barrier—had much delayed suburban growth and consequently park and planning policies as well. Because of the topography, the few extant parks in Virginia resembled concentric circles rather than distinct wedges. Major corridors of settlement as outlined by the Year 2000 Plan would occur along Interstate 95 toward the United States Marine Base at Quantico, in Prince William County, and along Interstate 66 toward Manassas. Well-defined green wedges could be found only along the Potomac River, both north and south of Washington. Thus, while the Maryland counties found the plan readily adaptable to their present situation of settlement, the Virginia counties accepted it in principle but found greater difficulties in adapting its configurations into their own long-range planning. In the actual adoption and implementation of the wedges and corridors, a regional planning basis would prove necessary. At present, this responsibility falls into the purview of the Council of Governments. Although not as yet possessed of any strong planning powers, the council has an active concern for consideration of the wedges plan in light of Metro construction and other re-evaluations.

Refocusing on the city within the District's boundaries, the NCPC issued a staff draft proposal for review and comment in 1965: "Proposed Physical Development Policies for the District of Columbia." This so-called "Brown Book" was described as "a resource paper" and was issued largely at the urging of the commission's new chairman, Mrs. Elizabeth Rowe, who wanted a substantial statement of commission policy proposals to which elements of the Washington community could respond. The statement also reflected the rapid growth in the period 1961–65 of what might be described as "community consciousness," deliberately fostered by the Washington Planning and Housing Association, and formalized in a study by the consultant Henry Bain. Unlike the Policies Plan which had invited only generalized response, the 1965 "Brown Book," prepared under the direction of William Dutton, was conceived to encourage the major agencies concerned with planning and with specific geographical sections of the city to make their views known. Its varied success in this attempt disclosed the problems of a voteless capital city not as yet accustomed to such expressions of interest. In what was becoming known as the Shaw neighborhood, and in the northeast section of Washington generally, for example, there was little response. Nevertheless, the "Brown Book" was an important step toward the publication in 1967 of a succeeding document.

Substantively the 1965 plan projected what the physical city would look like twenty years hence, in 1985. New values were offered. The urban identity was defined by its historic buildings and places, distinctive locales, special streets, entrances, and city edges, all laid over a more historically sophisticated interpretation of the natural topography. Revising somewhat the earlier proposed location of federal agencies along corridors, the NCPC in this plan suggested that the majority of federal agencies within the District of Columbia be located within the boundaries of the old L'Enfant city. New sites for public buildings were to be located along South Capitol Street and the Naval Weapons Plant, near the conjunction of New York Avenue and Eleventh Street, NW, and in several uptown locations, e.g., at the National Bureau of Standards' vacated site along Connecticut Avenue. Thus, the downtown would be reinforced as a compact central employment area and commercial center.

A still stronger environmental, community, and social context was offered in the NCPC's 1967 Proposed Comprehensive Plan for the National Capital. Known as the "Green Book," the 1967 report on the Comprehensive Plan was a more detailed, explicit proposal of elements in the plan, most of which had been announced in the earlier reports. Indeed, there were some readers who criticized the document as being too explicit, too tightly planned, too much concerned with the physical city. Yet, by providing target information, especially dates by which certain elements of the plan were to be realized, William Dutton's successor as executive director of the commission, Charles H. Conrad, succeeded in providing an important stimulus to planning by the agencies in the community whose response was important to the realization of the plan. As this plan was far more inclusive than any of the city's earlier plans, so was there reflected a corresponding desire on the part of the National Capital Planning Commission to include more consequential community participation.

In the specifics of the 1967 report, the city's natural topography was given greater definition. This was further amplified by a commission study of a comprehensive landscape plan for Washington. Communities were defined not only by natural features and functional characteristics but also by their architectural settings. These "existing physical plants" plus a careful planning for public services—schools, libraries, fire and police protection—could be used to give communities a strong physical identity. In the emphasis on community identity, the plan called for a downplaying of highways along with an upgrading of a balanced transportation system and the acceptance of congestion at peak hours.

Successive plans of the commission demonstrated that a dialogue between the NCPC and the Washington community had been successfully launched and was continuing as the mainstream of planning activity. This is a significant methodological departure from plans developed by experts and offered to the community on a "take it or leave it" basis, or prepared, like the 1950 and 1965 plans, primarily to satisfy some federal agency requirement. The sense of continuity in planning was revealed in frequent references to the "planning process" rather than "just making plans." An important response was being experienced by the city to a movement which in one way or another was refashioning city planning throughout the nation. These changes strongly reflected the views of Charles Conrad, the commission's executive director. As one result, the legitimacy and political force of the planning recommendations was greatly strengthened. In 1968 the proposed plan was presented to the commission for adoption.

Thus far, three elements of the Comprehensive Plan have been adopted since 1968. First, in the area of land use, the NCPC recommended that the open character of the city, that unique measure of the area's quality of life, be maintained against pressures for more intensive development, and that new development be oriented to an all-hour use of the city. New development was also to be harmonized with the area's unique physical features. Residential density would be highest just north of the central employment core and in other specified independent employment centers, encouraging business and governmental efficiency and walk-to-work living patterns. Areas of medium residential densities were projected as a transition between the extremes of high and low density sections of the city. Second, local recreation facilities were to be brought up to par with the national parks in the city and viewed as focal points for the local community. These recreational parks, intended primarily for the resident population, were to average two acres per 1000 in population. The gradations of local parks ranged from the District center, to intermediate community centers associated with schools, to small neighborhood centers. Third, the NCPC restated its past commitment to a balanced transportation system, the improvement of existing thoroughfare systems, and the planning for automobile parking at fringe locations and in the central area, all elements approved by the City Council. Future transportation planning was to be related to development and land use, thereby necessitating close cooperation with new public buildings programs.

Perhaps it could have been predicted that the parts of the plan the commission found of greatest federal significance—the land use, highways, and parks and recreation elements—were those most deeply rooted in the commission's historical activities. These were the elements to which the most study had been given, and with which the commission consequently was most familiar. These it adopted. The parts on which action was deferred—the sections of intense local concern dealing with residential development, housing, schools, and supporting facilities—posed important new questions and frequently involved conflicts with other operating agencies and their supporting federal program requirements. Nevertheless, this was the important day of reckoning for the commission. The result of its decisions was published in 1968 and, continuing the chromatic characterization of the preceding reports, was called the "Red Book." This was the initial step in a continuous effort, from 1968 on, to secure the adoption of other elements in the Comprehensive Plan.

In support of the adoption of elements of the Comprehensive Plan was the growing appreciation of the importance of these goals. There was, moreover, the realization that decisions concerning land use planning and the physical plan of the city reflected important economic and political assumptions—indeed, assumptions concerning the quality of life and other less measurable characteristics of the city. Taken into account also was the insistence of federal agencies that the programs they aided in such fields as transportation or housing be elements in more general plans. Given these pressures, planning continued to advance, especially in such critical sectors as transportation. The planning process has also helped the city face one of its major turnabouts: the problem of urban growth.

The land use objectives proposed in 1968 first enunciated the needs of a city of 840,000 population, far less than the zoning regulations could accommodate. By accepting these limits to future growth, and the low densities they implied, it became possible to make assumptions concerning the quality of life that such a city might offer. Thus, in step with the increasing concern with environmental quality, the NCPC raised the essential questions that had to be resolved.

The NCPC's plans for the residential city as a linking together of communities with strong social and physical identities were abetted by concomitant sectoral and project planning. Work on historic landmarks, focal points of unique places and communities, was adopted in 1965 by the Joint Committee on Landmarks sponsored by the National Capital Planning Commission, the Commission of Fine Arts, and later the District government. Interest in the city's historic buildings and places had already been expressed by the NCPC in its planning for the retention of a residential atmosphere for Lafayette Square. A strong central core was defined by the strengthened monumental groupings of public buildings: new museums and gardens along the Mall and the proposed Civic Center along Eighth Street as outlined in the NCPC staff report, "Downtown Design and Development Plan." A new mixed use for the National Airport and the Bolling Air Force Base as well as the transition in uses of other facilities along the city's two major rivers inspired—in 1972—the staff report, "The Urban River."

The regional planning functions, which since 1952 had been executed by the National Capital Regional Planning Council, were transferred in 1966 to the Metropolitan Washington Council of Governments, popularly known as COG. Whereas the Regional Planning Council had represented the area's planning bodies, and in part elected officials, COG represented all of the political bodies in the region. While planning thus acquired greater immediacy and clout, there was also a perceptible tendency to refer certain planning considerations to local jurisdictions. Thus, in the treatment of the proposals of the radial corridor plan, COG has deferred to local jurisdictions the development of definitive contributions towards the evolution of this 1961 concept.

The shape of modern Washington has also been dictated by redevelopment. In the procedure outlined by the District of Columbia Redevelopment Act of 1945, the National Capital Park and Planning Commission in a bicameral relationship with the District of Columbia government was authorized to designate redevelopment areas and boundaries, and to prepare and adopt plans in harmony with standing comprehensive plans. The newly

*Streets, 1942. Characterized by deteriorated
slums and modest row houses along tree-
lined streets, the crowded and decayed condition of the Southwest inspired calls for a
massive renewal. In the early 1950s, renewal
efforts resulted in removal of the area's population. The face of the old neighborhood
gave way to high-rise apartment buildings,
new row houses of a larger "Georgetown
townhouse" scale, and a marked alteration
of L'Enfant's street system.*

created Redevelopment Land Agency (RLA) was charged with the implementation of the NCPPC plans. Redevelopment had already captured the attention of the NCPPC as early as the mid-1940s when Marshall Heights and
Barry Farms, both in outlying sections of Anacostia, were considered and
proposed as prime target areas—although these proposed projects were never
funded by Congress. After passage of the Housing Act of 1949 stipulating
that no funding would be applied to areas previously proposed but not approved, the NCPPC turned to the inner city and particularly to the southwest
quadrant of the old city, identified by the 1950 Comprehensive Plan as a
"problem area."

The course of redevelopment in the Southwest was directed by the philosophy that the way to rid the city of slums was to remove all their physical

vestiges (figure 27). Plans for the Southwest prepared in 1952 for the NCPC by Elbert Peets urged, to the contrary, the retention and rehabilitation of existing buildings. Determining, however, that Peets's plan did not meet the legal requirements for redevelopment, the RLA commissioned a new plan prepared by architect-planners Louis Justement and Chloethiel Woodard Smith. This plan subsequently was adopted by the NCPPC and the District government. Guided by the need to attract middle-income families back to the inner city, the plan sought to include medium to moderate density housing, to provide a cross section of housing types and styles, and to encourage home ownership. Looking to the preserved and prosperous residential area of Georgetown where blight has been overcome, planners attempted to create the same ambience of townhouses with intimate gardens in the Southwest even if three-fourths of the new population were to live in apartments.

Although the radical redevelopment plans epitomized by the Southwest left some reminders of its past community in the preservation of a handful of historical structures and in the retention of some public housing, the need to phase relocation with the construction of new public housing in southeast Washington and Anacostia—as well as questions raised about creating a community in an all-new setting—led redevelopment planners to consider alternative solutions to inner-city slums. The 1954 Housing Act addressed these problems by allowing funding to be applied to the rehabilitation of existing structures, thus offering the potential for neighborhood conservation and the preservation of artifacts from the city's past.

The rehabilitation brand of redevelopment then shaped designated renewal areas of the city after the mid-1950s, most notably Foggy Bottom (figure 28) with its gasworks, brewery, lumberyards, and industry, situated between Washington's West End and fashionable Georgetown. Here, many older working-class houses were renewed in the Georgetown style, and new mixed and all-day use created packaged living complexes, such as Columbia Plaza and Watergate. The measure of federal aid received by Columbia Plaza was typical of this transitional period. Crowning the new Foggy Bottom, the national cultural center—the John F. Kennedy Center for the Performing Arts—successfully attracted a new clientele. Redevelopment areas were also designated in the northwest and northeast quadrants, many on a small-scale basis, carrying with them the meshing of rehabilitation and new construction and responding to the goals of urban and social continuity.

The 1960s witnessed other new approaches to the city's physical future. Dismayed by the blighted appearance of the north side of Pennsylvania Avenue (figure 29), President Kennedy created the President's Council on Pennsylvania Avenue to plan for the resurrection of the avenue as worthy of

63

FIGURE 28. *New Foggy Bottom, 1966. The expressway approaches to the new Theodore Roosevelt Bridge invaded Foggy Bottom's residential streets, and the large structures containing offices, hotels, and apartments increasingly dominated the earlier scale set by the area's row houses which had been built for the artisans of Hamburg. Key of Keys (Observatory Hill), one of Washington's earliest historic sites, here looks upon the construction of the Kennedy Center and Columbia Plaza, while in the distance the initial structures of the Watergate complex are seen.*

Washington Post *photograph.*

the capital city and the ceremonial functions it embraced. Kennedy also rescued Lafayette Square from McMillanism and office building efficiency, shelving plans for a tall executive office building design in favor of a design that preserved the residential character of the square and the White House. The retention of the red brick façades inspired John Carl Warnecke's two federal office buildings facing each other across the square, focusing on the contrast between the white-classical and the red-bricked traditions in public architecture. The preservation impulse was extended under President John-

FIGURE 29. *Pennsylvania Avenue Development Corporation Model Showing Updated Design, 1969. The ceremonial route had become a deteriorated commercial street, prompting new plans for future development. Accepting the trend in the area toward large-bulk office buildings with uniform cornice lines, this plan offered a solution to the "spoiled" view of the White House from the Capitol. This solution was in part accomplished with the proposed National Square (top center of picture).*

Photograph by Dwain Faubion.

son's administration around past the Blair-Lee Houses to the French Renaissance–styled old Court of Claims Building, rehabilitated to serve as the Smithsonian's Renwick Gallery.

Historic preservation, popularized in Georgetown, inspired other ventures in the changing regional city. Capitol Hill, not yet benefiting from the congressionally designated "historic district" status that endowed Georgetown with special protections, is being restored largely by vigorous private efforts. Alexandria, once the focus of President Washington's urban interests and loyalties, reflected a similar dilemma of the affluent, educated classes' moving in, raising real estate values beyond the means of the earlier indigenous population. The success of these refurbished neighborhoods as measured visually in new paint and new inhabitants obscured the less pleasant results of the higher rents that forced out the poor and transient into other sections of the city. Less important from an architectural standpoint, old streetcar and railroad suburbs—like Rockville, Maryland (figure 24), and Clifton, Virginia—represented preservation spurred by private individuals who were attracted by the vernacular qualities of the townscape. Interest in the preservation of old neighborhoods and towns, while often presenting unresolved social conflicts, turned the tide against renewal equaling removal. Renewal could now be defined as the retention and renovation of old structures.

As the regional city now regenerates its old settlements, formerly simple concepts such as open space, parks, neighborhoods, transportation routes, business districts, and employment centers, call for redefinition. Planning now entails the larger consideration of environmental quality, social planning, economic planning, political planning, the recognition of historical and scenic values, and many more aspects than ever imagined by the city's founders or, indeed, by its planners of more recent years. No doubt the creation of a District of Columbia planning office, as an accompaniment of municipal home rule, will call for some new priorities in planning for the city. The federal interest and coordination role in the capital city—this still its fundamental reason for being and the major determinant of its character as a physical city—has been reaffirmed as the principal responsibility of the National Capital Planning Commission. The future of the regional city is also affected by more than the sum of its present planning agencies. It will be determined by sustained redevelopment, the vast network of agency and individual decisions made in the piecemeal evolution of the physical city, by the new mass transportation system and the consequences of the Beltway, by Potomac environmental matters, and by the growth of a more formidable, private, Metro-oriented business community than Washington has known.

The tenth anniversary, in 1975, of the introduction of federal agency master plans found four-fifths of all federal installations in Washington covered by such plans. This significant move constituted both an important step for the capital city and a new application of planning powers. Correspondingly, the role of the National Capital Planning Commission in reviewing the capital budget programs of each federal department before these programs were submitted to the review of the Office of Management and Budget further strengthened the planning process. Such developments helped define the distinctive federal interest in the capital city and thus contributed to the newly defined role of the National Capital Planning Commission following the advent of a form of municipal home rule for the District of Columbia in 1974.

Historical Panorama: Two Centuries of Planning

The modern City of Washington has emerged as the outcome of nearly two centuries of systematic city-building efforts. As the outstanding example of an American planned city and the symbolic planned capital of the nation, metropolitan Washington is spread over nearly 5,000 square miles. The built city now includes four suburban counties and bits of other counties in both Maryland and Virginia. In the growth of the city as a whole, mainly since 1933, the District of Columbia has "shrunk" to less than the size of a municipal postage stamp on a regional letter. But the ancient capital, L'Enfant's city, was a precious city, a mature city, a horizontal city, crowded with history and monuments, outstanding public buildings and symbolic architecture (figure 30). It was, above all, a green city set in the carefully designed landscape of river meadows, wooded terraces and ravines, formal parks, tree-lined avenues, and natural features. It had established itself in the affections of the nation. And it has been an active city, visited annually by tens of millions of persons. Their business was to do with federal agencies and the more than a thousand national organizations, associations, and professional societies that make their headquarters here. A hundred thousand students attended its internationally known universities. Among these millions of visitors to the City of Washington were tourists from every corner of the nation and world, drawn here by the fascination of current events no less than by historical associations and the wealth of artistic, literary, historical, and scientific objects that crowd the city's libraries and museums. It was a city whose image on television filled screens throughout the world. Yet, enjoying as well the fruits of careful planning and the thoughtful benefits of those who had expressed their love for the place in gifts of parkland or landmarks and institutions like Dumbarton Oaks, the city possessed features to be discovered in season by its own residents as well as by those with more than a day or two to visit. The bustle and stir of Paris and London, business and financial as well as political capitals, had at last come to Washington in the age of mass communication, international economic organization, and office building enterprises. Like other urban centers, Washington too responded to national characteristics of mobility, leisure, affluence, and growth. It dealt with these new conditions with a greater care to recognize values from the past and with the assurance and experience in planning that had accumulated during the entire lifetime of the city.

Above all, it is to the future that the City of Washington looks, as it has looked for two centuries. In terms of the future it is responding to new urban goals and issues, to questions of social justice, to environmental quality, to the change generated by the expanding metropolis of which it is the center, as well as by expanding urban functions and federal needs. And in contemplating the future, the planned city continues to find its most fundamental role as the National Capital.

Bibliographical Notes

Several imaginative annotated bibliographies have been published in recent years. See Perry C. Fisher, *Materials for the Study of Washington* (Washington, D.C., 1974), for incisive commentary on a wide range of books about the city; and Anne Llewellyn Meglis, *D.C. Redevelopment Land Agency Presents a Bibliographic Tour of Washington, D.C.* (Washington, D.C., 1974), for works emphasizing the physical city and urban planning. The National Capital Planning Commission, *Bibliography of Studies and Reports of the District of Columbia and the Washington Metropolitan Area* (Washington, D.C., 1967), provides a listing useful for specialized and contemporary insights into the city.

For manuscript sources, the National Archives Record Group 42, Section 328, contains the records of the National Capital Park and Planning Commission, comprising 377 boxes arranged according to subjects and dates. Comparable records of the Commission of Fine Arts are in Record Group 42, Section 66. Published official reports of District and federal agencies are of particular value. Special collections of historical material, including classified newspaper articles and much iconographical material, are maintained by the Washingtoniana Division of the Martin Luther King Memorial Library, the Columbia Historical Society, and the Prints and Photographs Division of the Library of Congress.

Topographical detail is provided by the series of maps associated with the L'Enfant Plan—L'Enfant's "manuscript map" (1791), the engraved plan by Ellicott (1791), the Boschke plan of 1856—all of which may be consulted in the Geography and Map Division of the Library of Congress. See also the Engineer Commissioner's plans for street extensions (1895, 1897), at the National Archives; the plans incorporated in the published report of the McMillan Commission (1902); and the numerous maps and plans published in the annual reports of the National Capital Park and Planning Commission and in the comprehensive plans and special planning reports subsequently issued, as identified in the text. For a long-range iconographical study, see Chalmers M. Roberts, *Washington, Past and Present* (Washington, D.C., 1949–50).

Washington's standard general histories are Wilhelmus B. Bryan, *A History of the National Capital*, 2 vols. (New York, 1914–16), and Constance McLaughlin Green, *Washington*, 2 vols. (Princeton, 1963–64). An indispensable reference collection is the *Records of the Columbia Historical Society*, published since 1894 in 48 volumes to 1971–72.

Washington's physical identity has been formed out of a unique set of topographical features upon which man-made creations were fashioned. See the

The Washington Plan

National Capital Planning Commission, *Toward a Comprehensive Landscape Plan for Washington, D.C.* (Washington, D.C., 1967), for an inquiry into this identity. The city's most distinctive environmental feature, merging together a vast and complex region, is explored in Frederick Gutheim, *The Potomac* (New York, 1949). John W. Reps, *Tidewater Towns* (Williamsburg, 1972), describes for comparison the growth of human settlements along the southern reaches of the Potomac and other tidal inlets. A history of the ceremonial and governmental core of the city is presented in John W. Reps, *Monumental Washington* (Princeton, 1967). References to Washington within the framework of the history of city planning in the United States are found in Mel Scott, *American City Planning Since 1890*, 2d edn. (Berkeley, 1971). Antedating the founding of the capital city, the region had already produced unique architectural features, as described in Thomas T. Waterman, *The Mansions of Virginia 1706–1776* (Chapel Hill, 1946) and *The Dwellings of Colonial America* (Chapel Hill, 1950). Specialized architectural references are gathered in Mary Lethbridge and Donald F. Lethbridge, "A Washington Bookshelf," *Journal of the American Institute of Architects* 39 (January 1963): 117–18.

1790–1800, Designing the City The biographies of L'Enfant tend to be compendious in form but valuable documents have been collected in H. Paul Caemmerer, *The Life of Pierre Charles L'Enfant* (Washington, D.C., 1950), and Elizabeth S. Kite, *L'Enfant and Washington* (Baltimore, 1929). Lively analyses of the unfinished plan and its immediate successor versions are offered in Paul D. Spreiregen, ed., *On the Art of Designing Cities: Selected Essays of Elbert Peets* (Cambridge, Mass., 1968), and William Partridge, *L'Enfant's Methods and Features of His Plan for the Federal City* (Washington, D.C., 1930; reprint edn., National Capital Planning Commission, 1975). For insight into the European influences on L'Enfant's work, see Helen Rosenau, *The Ideal City* (London, 1959), and Helen M. Fox, *André Le Nôtre: Garden Architect to Kings* (New York, 1962).

1800–1860, The Port City There are many descriptions of life in the early city that reflect its rapid environmental changes. See especially Margaret Bayard Smith, *The First Forty Years of Washington Society* (New York, 1906). Daniel D. Reiff presents the architectural developments during this period, in *Washington Architecture, 1791–1861: Problems in Development* (Washington, D.C., 1971), but under the heavy hand of a "creative immaturity" thesis. The considerable talents of nationally prominent architects in the city are documented in Helen Mar Pierce Gallagher, *Robert Mills* (New York, 1935), and Talbot Hamlin, *Benjamin Henry Latrobe* (New York, 1955). For the effects of the early development of the town on national politics and local lifestyles, see James Sterling Young, *The Washington Community, 1800–1828* (New York, 1966). Wilhelmus B. Bryan, *A History of the National Capital,* mentioned earlier, develops the theme of the indecisiveness of governmental commitment to the city, as seen in public works projects and the responding to emergency conditions rather than to an over-all plan.

1860–1865, The Civil War

Margaret Leech, *Reveille in Washington* (New York, 1941), offers a vivid history of the city divided between regional sympathies. See also Stanley Kimmel, *Mr. Lincoln's Washington* (New York, 1957), for a heavily pictorial account of the fortress city; and Mary Mitchell, *Divided Town* (Barre, Mass., 1968), for a localized account of Georgetown's response to the national crisis.

1865–1900, The Postbellum City

The annual reports of the Chief of Engineers on from 1867, when the Army Corps of Engineers took primary responsibility for the planning and beautification of the city, offer a continuous drama of Army Engineers' efforts to modernize the city, to make it floodproof and healthy, to provide the social amenities of parks and recreation, and to retain and develop historical properties in the area. Many of the major concerns (e.g., reclamation of the flats, water supply) are here provided with historical dimensions. An analysis of the Corps's long-overlooked role in the Victorian city is presented in Albert E. Cowdrey, *Design for a City: The U.S. Army Engineers in the Building of the Nation's Capital* (MS, Historical Division, Office of the Chief of Engineers, 1974). Paul O. McQueen traces the Corps's contributions in providing the city with a clean and adequate water supply, in *The Washington Aqueduct, 1852–1952* (MS, Washington District, Corps of Engineers, 1953). A cipher of changing aims in the appearance of the city is investigated in Joanna Schneider Zangrando, "Monumental Bridge Design in Washington, D.C. as a Reflection of American Culture, 1886–1932" (Ph.D. dissertation, George Washington University, 1974). The short-lived but indelible career of Alexander R. Shepherd and the Board of Public Works is explored in William Maury, *Alexander "Boss" Shepherd and the Board of Public Works* (Washington, D.C., 1975), where the dual theses of the investments concentrated in the northwest quadrant and Shepherd's friends as financial beneficiaries are explored. For a personalized view of the transformed city's influencing a larger region, see Samuel C. Busey, *Pictures of the City of Washington in the Past* (Washington, D.C., 1898), and *Personal Reminiscences* (Washington, D.C., 1895).

1900–1926, The Metropolitan City

The opening act of this period, the work and report of the McMillan Commission, is documented in U.S., Congress, Senate, Committee on the District of Columbia, *The Improvement of the Park System of the District of Colum-*

bia, 57th Cong., 1st sess., 1902, S. Rep. 166. For a detailed account of the commission's work, see John W. Reps, *Monumental Washington,* mentioned previously. An excellent professional and personal study of the plan's chief mover is developed in Thomas S. Hines, *Burnham of Chicago* (New York, 1974), which dramatically reinterprets Burnham beyond the standard study offered earlier in Charles Moore, *Daniel H. Burnham, Architect, Planner of Cities,* 2 vols. (Boston and New York, 1921). Biographical studies of other members of the commission include Charles Moore, *The Life and Times of Charles Follen McKim* (Boston, 1929); Charles Lewis Hind, *Augustus Saint-Gaudens* (New York, 1908); and Louise Tharp, *Saint-Gaudens and the Gilded Era* (Boston, 1969).

The annual reports of the Chief of Engineers again provide a comprehensive view of the work of the Army Engineers in planning and implementing necessary public works and recreational amenities. An encyclopedic analysis of the gracious Washington architecture along Massachusetts Avenue is presented in the U.S. Commission of Fine Arts, *Massachusetts Avenue Architecture,* 2 vols. (Washington, D.C., 1973–75). See also the minutes of the National Capital Park Commission and the annual reports of the Commission of Fine Arts.

1926–1976, The Regional City and The Continuing Plan Highlights in the voluminous literature of this period include annual reports, minutes, and publications of the National Capital Park and Planning Commission (1926–52) and the National Capital Planning Commission (1952–). For the earlier years in this period, see chapters on Washington in the *American Planning and Civic Annual, 1929–48.* See also the hearings, reports, and documents of the Joint Committee on Washington Metropolitan Problems (1958–59); Harold Lewis, *Rezoning Studies of the District of Columbia* (1956); the report of the President's Council on Pennsylvania Avenue (Washington, D.C., 1964); and the report of the President's Temporary Commission on Pennsylvania Avenue (Washington, D.C., 1967). A history of redevelopment in the city can be traced in the annual reports of the Redevelopment Land Agency as well as in its special studies, documents, and files. The development of metropolitan government and planning agencies in the region can be traced through the annual reports of the Metropolitan Washington Council of Governments, the documents of the Maryland–National Capital Park and Planning Commission, and the documents of the Fairfax County and Arlington County planning bodies.

THE EXHIBITION

THE FEDERAL CITY: PLANS & REALITIES

WILCOMB E. WASHBURN

Director, Office of American Studies, Smithsonian Institution
President, Columbia Historical Society

Contents

74

THE FEDERAL CITY

WASHINGTON, OUR CAPITAL CITY, WAS CREATED—AS WAS OUR CONSTITUTION—by an act of faith and reason. Both qualities were necessary to establish the location of the city and to support the grand plan that determined its form. Both the federal city and the federal government utilized European precedents. Yet, both were influenced by the American environment. As the founders believed, and as the motto on the Great Seal of the United States says, they were creating a "novus ordo seclorum," a new order in the world.

The purpose of this exhibition is to show graphically and spatially how the city was planned. It deals in particular with the 1791 neoclassical master plan of Pierre L'Enfant, the 1851 informal landscape plan of Andrew Jackson Downing, the 1902 formalistic plan of the Senate Park Commission, and the present humanistically oriented planning of the National Capital Planning Commission, the Pennsylvania Avenue Development Corporation, the National Park Service, the Commission of Fine Arts, and the District government. The exhibition concentrates particularly on Washington's central monumental core.

Locating Washington

The choice of the Potomac, and specifically the present District of Columbia, was the result of a complicated maneuver in which public and private as well as sectional interests were inextricably brought together. A Potomac location was strongly desired by the Virginians Washington, Jefferson, and Madison. They saw the Potomac River as the logical western pathway to the vast resources of the interior beyond the Appalachian Mountains. They feared that westerners might seek independence (or connections with other nations) if frustrated by an inappropriate location of the new capital or by other decisions against their interests. They sought to overcome Virginia opposition to the federal government—from dissenters like George Mason—by emphasizing the personal gains to them should the new capital be located near their lands. The danger of a capital on tidewater, accessible to hostile foreign fleets, was recognized by all but discounted by President Washington who felt the danger overemphasized.

The debate on where to locate the capital was joined in the summer of 1790. The forces favoring a Potomac location proposed that the site be chosen from an area between the Eastern Branch (later called the Anacostia River) and the Conococheague Creek, adjoining Pennsylvania near the village of Hancock. Support for the Potomac location required a temporary alliance between Virginia and Pennsylvania and was finally achieved through a com-

FIGURE 30. *View of Washington from Arlington National Cemetery, 1975.* In this view of the city from Arlington toward the east, the tomb of Pierre Charles L'Enfant, "Engineer, Artist, Soldier," is shown in the foreground.

Photograph by Staples & Charles.

promise proposed by Secretary of the Treasury Alexander Hamilton. In this compromise, a bill by which the federal government would assume the debts contracted by the states during the American Revolution was supported by Virginia and Maryland congressmen in exchange for votes for the Potomac location by congressmen from Pennsylvania.

Once the "residence bill" establishing the location of the capital became law, there was a further struggle over the precise location of the ten-mile square federal District. President Washington was authorized to determine the site at any point on the Potomac between tidewater and the Pennsylvania line. Although he visited potential upriver sites just prior to his final decision, Washington had decided early on locating the capital at the junction of tidewater and piedmont (figure 1). Despite the proximity of the designated federal District to George Washington's estate at Mount Vernon, such was the president's known probity and reputation that no serious suggestion of self-interest has ever been imputed to him. On 24 January 1791, the president issued a proclamation establishing the seat of government and defining its general outline. At the same time he sent a message to Congress suggesting an amendment to the Residence Act to allow the southeastern boundary of the District to include territory in Maryland below the Anacostia River, as well as the town of Alexandria in Virginia. Congress approved the suggestion and by proclamation, on 30 March 1791, the new boundaries were formally defined by President Washington. The generous proportions of the ten-mile square designated as the federal District exceeded the vision of a later generation of legislators who, in 1846, returned the Virginia portion of the District to that state.

For further historical details, see "Washington Panorama," the opening section of this book. Also consult the bibliography for the exhibition and the index, at the back of the book.

PLANNING WASHINGTON

Pierre L'Enfant the Man

The person selected by President George Washington to lay out the new capital was Pierre L'Enfant. Major L'Enfant was a French military engineer who had served gallantly with the American forces during the Revolution. After the Revolution, L'Enfant made his living in the new republic as an engineer and architect in New York City, where he was chosen to remodel Federal Hall, the temporary seat of the new government. He thus became a familiar figure to the leaders of the new nation.

L'Enfant was expected to work under the general direction of three commissioners appointed to oversee the building of the federal city. L'Enfant considered the work to be his personal and exclusive responsibility, however, and repeatedly disregarded advice and instructions given him by the commissioners. In one rash incident, L'Enfant ordered a new house of the nephew of one of the commissioners (Daniel Carroll) to be torn down because it projected a few feet over the line L'Enfant had plotted to mark out New Jersey Avenue, SE. Distressed by this and many similar incidents, Carroll and his fellow commissioners insisted to President Washington that L'Enfant had to go, unless he would subordinate himself to them. He refused. In February 1792, Washington dismissed the fiery genius.

BASIC CHARACTERISTICS OF THE L'ENFANT PLAN: L'Enfant's plan for the new federal city expresses in physical form the concept of separation of powers and balanced federal-state relations created by the new Constitution. The Capitol was located on the most prominent elevation, Jenkins Hill, which L'Enfant, in his reconnaissance of the area, had described as "a pedestal waiting for a monument." A great ceremonial avenue, four hundred feet in width to be lined with imposing houses and gardens, was plotted due west from the Capitol to the site of a proposed monument of George Washington on horseback. Another great avenue (Pennsylvania Avenue) ran diagonally from the Capitol northwest to an elevated site, due north of the proposed Washington Monument, where L'Enfant located the President's House. Pennsylvania Avenue represented the connection as well as the separation of the legislative and executive branches of government.

Throughout the rest of the federal city, L'Enfant placed a system of broad diagonal avenues over a conventional grid system of streets. Squares and circles evenly spaced throughout the grid were designed as focal points for local communities reflecting the interests of the several states of the Union. Many of these communities were joined to each other by broad diagonal avenues, which provided the most direct physical link between points of the grid. The number of diagonals was reduced and certain minor changes made by Andrew Ellicott, who was appointed to make the detailed survey of the District and complete the map of the District after L'Enfant's dismissal.

78

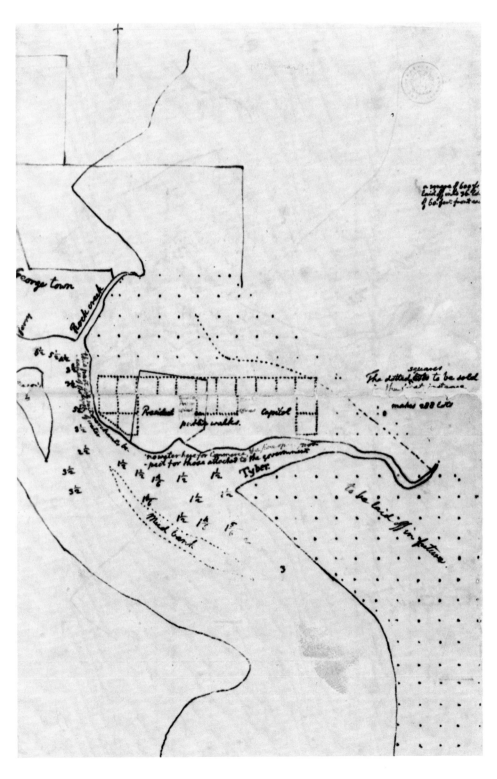

FIGURE 32. *Miniature of Andrew Ellicott.*
Courtesy Museum of History and Technology, Smithsonian Institution.

THE SURVEY OF THE DISTRICT OF COLUMBIA: President Washington and Secretary of State Jefferson (figure 31), both experienced surveyors, "were the real delineators of the federal District," in the words of scholar Julian Boyd. The surveyor Andrew Ellicott (figure 32) was chosen to run the precise boundaries. During some portion of his labors Ellicott was assisted by Benjamin Banneker, a free black whose grandmother was white. Authorities still disagree sharply about Banneker's role in the survey of the federal city (figure 2). Boyd thinks "there is no evidence whatever that Banneker had anything to do with the survey of the federal city." On the other hand, Silvio Bedini, biographer of Banneker, asserts that Banneker played a significant role as Ellicott's scientific assistant.

NEGLECT AND CHANGE: L'Enfant's plan was so vast and comprehensive that it could not be immediately realized. Although it set the basic conditions for Washington's early growth, it was frequently modified and often unrealized. The Washington Canal, which was supposed to be an economic lifeline as well as an aesthetic spine, became neither. The Chesapeake & Ohio Canal, with which it was linked, failed to reach its own goal of tapping the rich trans-Appalachian West. Poor economic conditions, slow growth, and time itself (figure 6) combined to convince Congress and the city fathers that, as a commissioner of public buildings put it, "The plan of Washington, by avoiding one error may have run into the contrary extreme, and more space may have been reserved than it is necessary or expedient to retain." Congress, in accordance with this belief, by an act of 7 May 1822, relinquished to the city, for the purpose of "improvement," much of the eastern portion of the Mall along Pennsylvania Avenue and Maryland Avenue. The city canal route, as planned by L'Enfant, was realigned by Charles Bulfinch (making a sharp right turn near Fifth Street, NW, to the center of the Mall, where it turned due east) in order to facilitate the creating of saleable lots. The "waste" space, as the Mall had come to be regarded, was gradually converted into building lots along Pennsylvania and Maryland Avenues. Despite the efforts to spur growth, Washington continued in the economic doldrums. The city canal soon became filled more with trash than with boats (figure 9). The development of the Baltimore & Ohio Railroad in the late 1820s and 1830s spelled an end to Washington's hopes of tapping the wealth of the West by the canal route. By 1850, L'Enfant's vision of a Grand Avenue running down the Mall was set back further from realization when Congress authorized the Botanic Gardens to be located directly at the foot of Capitol Hill (figure 39).

Andrew Jackson Downing the Man

Andrew Jackson Downing (figure 33) was a horticulturist and the most distinguished landscape architect of his day. In 1850, he was asked by President Fillmore—at the urging of Joseph Henry, first Secretary of the Smithsonian—to bring beauty into the city that had largely forgotten L'Enfant's legacy. Like Pierre L'Enfant, Downing was a moody genius and often struggled with members of Congress, and with the commissioner of public buildings, who frequently challenged his ideas or sought to cut off his resources. There was much criticism of Downing's notion that it was necessary for him to come down to Washington from his home in Newburgh, New York, only periodically—to check progress and give occasional instructions. Although President Fillmore enthusiastically approved Downing's landscape plan, Congress provided the requested funds grudgingly and slowly. Downing's work had hardly begun to be implemented when he died tragically in a steamboat accident on the Hudson River. And after his death Congress killed further development of the plan by turning off funds.

FIGURE 33. *Andrew Jackson Downing. Photograph courtesy George B. Tatum.*

BASIC CHARACTERISTICS OF THE DOWNING ROMANTIC LANDSCAPE PLAN: Downing's plan has usually been called "romantic." He himself called it the "natural" style. Downing saw the Mall as a place of resort and recreation where residents of the city could enjoy not only nature but man's "improvement" of nature (figure 10). Downing sought to introduce many hitherto unfamiliar species of trees—particularly evergreens—into the Washington landscape, and to facilitate access by curving carriage and walking paths that would invite the visitor to refresh himself amidst the carefully cultivated beauty.

Downing did not ignore the significance of the Mall and Pennsylvania Avenue as symbolic elements in the over-all plan for the city. The monumental arch he planned for the White House terminus of Pennsylvania Avenue shows his recognition of that avenue's symbolic importance (figure 34). Yet, because his treatment of the two axes was less formal than that proposed by either L'Enfant or later planners, he is often charged with having ignored the significance of the axes.

Downing reinforced L'Enfant's idea of a canal city (figure 35). He designed, as an ornamental and practical addition linking the Mall and the President's Park, a suspension bridge strong enough for carriages to pass over and high enough for "vessels of moderate size to pass under" (figure 34). As late as 1930, the trees planted in accordance with Downing's 1851 plan dominated the Smithsonian section of the Mall, which Downing had labeled "Smithsonian Pleasure Grounds" (figure 5). Today only a few trees planted in accordance with Downing's plan remain to be seen on the Mall (figure 36).

Washington I propose to keep the large area of this ground open, as a place for parade or military reviews, as well as public festivities or celebrations. A circular carriage-drive, 40 feet wide, and nearly a mile long, shaded by an avenue of Elms, surrounds the Parade, while a series of foot-paths, 10 feet wide, winding through thickets of trees and shrubs, forms the boundary to this park, and would make an agreeable shaded promenade for pedestrians.—

I propose to take down the present small stone gates to the President's Grounds, and place at the end of Pennsylvania Avenue a large and handsome Archway of marble, which shall not only form the main entrance from the City to the whole of the proposed new Grounds, but shall also be one of the principal Architectural ornaments of the city; inside of this arch-way is a semicircle with three gates commanding three carriage-roads.—Two of these lead into the Parade or President's Park, the third is a private carriage-drive into the President's grounds; this gate should be protected by a Porter's lodge, and should only be open on reception days,

Presidents Arch
at the end of Penn? Avenue.

thus making the President's grounds on the side of the house quite private at all other times. I propose to have the _exit_ of guests on reception days on this side of the house, the _entrance_ now, on the other side. I have not shown on the plan several ideas that have occurred to me for increasing the beauty and seclusion of the President's grounds, because I would first wish to submit them for the approval of the President.

2nd   Monument Park.

This comprises the fine plot of ground surrounding the Washington monument and bordered by the Potomac. To reach it from the President's Park, I propose to cross the canal by a wire suspension bridge, sufficiently strong for carriages, which would permit vessels of moderate size to pass under it, and would be an ornamental feature in the grounds. I propose to plant Monument Park wholly with American trees, of large growth, disposed in open groups, so as to allow of fine vistas of the Potomac river.—

[Suspension bridge across the Canal]

THE SMITHSONIAN BUILDING: The building chosen to house the Federal City Exhibition was built in the 1850s as the first Smithsonian Building. Joseph Henry, first Secretary of the Smithsonian, was not happy with it. To Henry, the building was too elaborate for what he believed to be the Smithsonian's primary purposes, research and scholarly work, not display of museum collections or public lectures. "Much as I am an admirer of good building," he wrote, "I do not choose to be its victim." It was too costly a monument, he believed, to be allowed to absorb so large a portion of the one-half million dollar bequest of James Smithson. Smithson, illegitimate son of the Duke of Northumberland, had provided in his will "to found at Washington, under the name of the Smithsonian Institution, an establishment for the increase and diffusion of knowledge among men."

FIGURE 35. *The United States Capitol, 1858. In this watercolor sketch by Joacim Ferdinand Richardt, the Washington Canal is shown* in the foreground.

Courtesy Political History Division of the Museum of History and Technology, Smithsonian Institution.

To increase the funds available for this purpose through the accumulation of interest on the one-half million dollars, Joseph Henry slowed construction during the early 1850s. The building was completed, however, in 1855—in the grand form Congress had mandated—to accommodate collections, exhibits, public lectures, and housing and offices for the scholarly staff. Joseph Henry and his family occupied quarters in the East Wing. His office was in the South Tower.

The American sculptor Horatio Greenough, on the evening of his arrival in Washington in 1851 after nine years' absence, found himself in approximately the spot from which Mathew Brady later took the picture shown in figure 37. "Suddenly, as I walked," Greenough wrote, "the dark form of the Smithsonian palace rose between me and the white Capitol, and I stopped."

Greenough's description is vivid:

> Tower and battlement, and all that medieval confusion, stamped itself on the halls of Congress, as ink on paper! Dark on that whiteness—complication on that simplicity! . . .
>
> "Bosom'd high in tufted trees," the Smithsonian College must, in itself, be hereafter a most picturesque object—the models whence it has been imitated are both "rich and rare"—the connoisseurs may well "wonder how the devil it got *there*."

85

James McMillan and the Senate Park Commission

The celebration in 1900 of the one hundredth anniversary of the move of the capital to Washington was the occasion for a new look at the Washington city plan. This new look came at the urging of the American Institute of Architects, which held its annual meeting in Washington during the Centennial celebration. Senator James McMillan, chairman of the Senate Committee on the District of Columbia, obtained Senate authorization for his committee to consider the potential development of Washington's park system and the designation of ideal locations for future public buildings. McMillan could not coordinate this move with the House of Representatives, which was adjourned; this later proved an embarrassment. The committee nevertheless established a planning commission, the Senate Park Commission, and moved rapidly ahead. The new commission consisted of four members: architect Daniel H. Burnham of Chicago (figure 38), landscape designer Frederick Law Olmsted, Jr., of Brookline, Massachusetts, architect Charles McKim of New York, and sculptor Augustus Saint-Gaudens of New York. Burnham was the driving force behind the commission in its dealings with Congress and the public. Like L'Enfant and Downing, Burnham insisted on ideal solutions and untrammeled authority, with compromise accepted only as a last resort.

FIGURE 38. *Daniel Hudson Burnham. Courtesy Library of Congress.*

THE MALL IN 1900: The 1901 model of the City of Washington (figure 39) prepared by the Senate Park Commission shows the Mall as it was at that time. By 1900, the city had slipped into incoherence and disorder owing to the lack of funds and coordinated planning, and the existence of independently administered districts and conflicting interests. The deterioration was most evident in the Mall area, which had become neither L'Enfant's "Grand Avenue" nor Downing's extended informal park. The model shows the fragmented results of many years' lack of planning or coordination, each department going its own way independently of the others. At the western end of the Mall (the bottom of the photograph shown in figure 39), between Fourteenth and Twelfth Streets, are the gardens of the Department of Agriculture. They front the department's old headquarters, replaced early in the twentieth century by the present Department of Agriculture Building. Between Twelfth and Seventh Streets are the Smithsonian "Pleasure Grounds," extending north of the Smithsonian Building. Between Seventh and Sixth Streets are the tracks and the station of the Pennsylvania Railroad. Between Sixth and Third Streets are the buildings, along Pennsylvania and Maryland Avenues, built in the formerly open Mall between 1820 and 1900. Between Third and First Streets are greenhouses and sheds belonging to the Botanic Gardens and authorized for construction at the foot of Capitol Hill in 1850.

86

FIGURE 39. *Three-dimensional Model of the City of Washington as It Existed in 1901. The western section of the Mall, near Fourteenth Street, is shown at the bottom of the photograph. Between Fourteenth and Twelfth Streets are the Department of Agriculture gardens. Between Twelfth and Seventh Streets are the Smithsonian "Pleasure Grounds." Between Seventh and Sixth Streets is the Pennsylvania Railroad station. Between Third and First Streets are the greenhouses and sheds of the Botanic Gardens.*

Courtesy Commission of Fine Arts.

FIGURE 44. *Three-dimensional Model of the Design Proposed by the Senate Park Commission for the Mall and Capitol Grounds, 1901–1902.*

Courtesy Commission of Fine Arts.

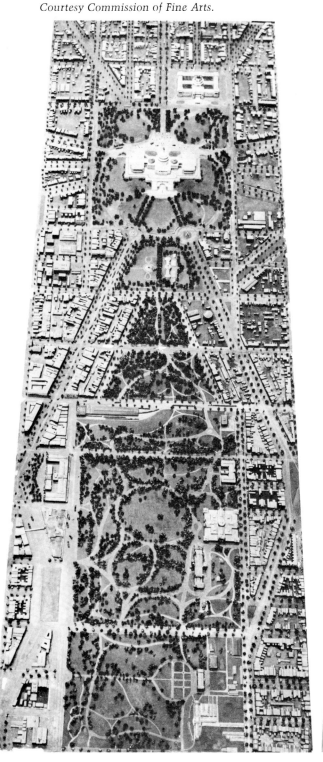

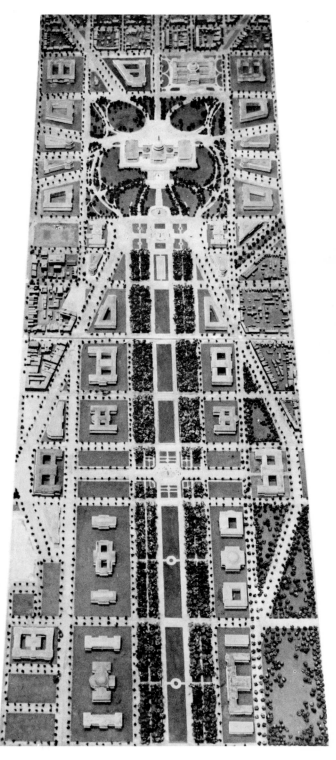

EUROPEAN INFLUENCES ON THE SENATE PARK COMMISSION: Three original members of the Senate Park Commission—Burnham, Olmsted, and McKim—in June and July of 1901 visited and photographed European cities whose plans might be significant to the further planning of Washington (figures 40, 41). While Daniel Burnham, the engine of the commission, felt that in Washington the "simplicity, directness and the subordination of ornamental structural uses" characteristic of Rome rather than Paris "should prevail," in fact Paris ultimately provided a more important model.

When the commission sought to obtain the agreement of President Cassatt of the Pennsylvania Railroad to move his station from the Mall, they envisaged bringing him to Paris with them, "and, standing on the terrace overlooking the Place de la Concorde, to take note of the glories of a city designed as a work of art—the Palace of the Tuileries as the Capitol, the Tuileries Gardens as the Mall, the Obelisk in the crossing of two Paris axes as the Washington Monument centers the Capitol and White House axes; and then a Lincoln Memorial as a national monument in location at the termination of the composition, and also as a center of distribution comparable to the Arc de Triomphe de l'Étoile." Yet, England also touched the imagination of the commission members and influenced their reinterpretation of the Mall in Washington.

THE PARK COMMISSION PLAN'S BASIC CHARACTERISTICS: The Senate Park Commission's principal achievement was to foster a system of parks extending throughout the limits of the original District of Columbia. This achievement was obscured—designedly to some degree—by the commission's spectacular plans for the central Mall area (figures 16, 17). Nevertheless, the plans to create an integrated park system throughout the Potomac, Anacostia, and Rock Creek watersheds has, in large measure, been realized.

While the Park Commission called for an "undulating" though formal greensward down the middle of the Mall, that central area as it slowly developed in the 1920s, '30s, and '40s was shaped into a nearly level space serving primarily to emphasize the formal link between the Washington Monument and the Capitol (figure 42). Along each side of the Mall four parallel rows of elms were planted, and large neoclassic buildings to house museums and semipublic institutions were erected. As Commission Chairman Burnham put it: "We do not feel that [the Mall] can with propriety be left in its natural state. We do not think that in the midst of a great city, which has formality all about it, that informality should become the rule. We think with the Capitol at one end and the Monument at the other, which are the most formal things in the world, the treatment between these structures should be equally formal."

FIGURE 40. *The Tuileries Gardens, Paris. This view along the major axis between the Arc du Carrousel and the Arc de Triomphe shows the obelisk marking the cross axis at the Place de la Concorde. Shown here is the photographic enlargement made by the Senate Park Commission for its 1902 exhibition.*

Courtesy Commission of Fine Arts.

FIGURE 41. *The Long Walk at Windsor, near London. This photographic enlargement made by the Senate Park Commission for the 1902 exhibition shows the undulating grassy mall. Frederick Law Olmsted, Jr., the landscape architect member of the commission, was strongly influenced by the informal English mall. Its influence—minus the central driveway at Windsor Great Park (shown here), to which he strongly objected—was felt in the design for the Mall in Washington.*

Courtesy Commission of Fine Arts.

FIGURE 42. *Aerial View of the Mall. This view looking east from the Washington Monument toward the Capitol shows the planting of four parallel rows of elm trees during the 1930s.*

Courtesy Commission of Fine Arts.

FIGURE 43. *Cartoon by Jim Berryman. This cartoon appeared in the* Washington Evening Star *on 14 January 1908. It is entitled, "Group of Le Notre-McKim Tree-Butchers and Nature-Butchers. Architect McKim, Architect Burnham, Architect Glenn Brown, Architect Green, Architect Hornblower, Architect Donn." The caption at the bottom reads: "The group of tree-butchers and nature-butchers depicted above are represented as on their way with axes to make a 'clean sweep,' as they proclaim, of all the grand old trees on the Mall. They are costumed on architectural straight lines. Architect McKim heads the party. He is blowing a big horn—his own. He also has a big head. Architect Donn will be recognized by his conceited upturned nose. In the rear are men bearing a great number of tubbed trees intended to replace the big trees destroyed. For further particulars inquire within." Photograph from the Library of Congress Newspaper Division, reprinted by permission of the* Washington Star.

There was no place in the Senate Park Commission's plan for the Smithsonian Building, designed by James Renwick, Jr., both because it projected too far into the Mall area and also because of its Victorian style, then out of favor. Although hearings in 1904 envisaged the removal—not the destruction—of the Smithsonian Institution Building behind the line sought to be cleared, it is difficult to determine whether this proposal was serious, or merely a sop thrown to the protopreservationists of the day. For even as late as 1931, the National Capital Park and Planning Commission, then principal planning agency of the District of Columbia, reaffirmed its support for the eventual removal of the Smithsonian Building in accordance with the Senate Park Commission Plan.

At the western terminus of the Mall, the Washington Monument anchored the vista from the Capitol. Elaborate sunken gardens proposed for the western side of the monument attempted to correct the off-center north-south axis from the White House. South of the monument were projected sites both for a principal memorial honoring the founding fathers and for facilities for indoor and outdoor sports.

THE PARK COMMISSION'S MODELS: In working out its plans, the Senate Park Commission found it necessary to have two models prepared, showing in accurate detail the central area of the City of Washington. One model showed *existing* conditions and the other, the *proposed* modifications (figures 39, 44). These models were made under the direction of George Carroll Curtis, geographical sculptor, of Boston. The models, along with colored architectural drawings and the photographs of European cities taken by the commissioners on their earlier trip, were exhibited during January and February, 1902, in the Corcoran Museum of Art—and later in the Library of Congress. Charles McKim, one of the commission members, spent the three days before the opening of the exhibition on a stepladder, hanging and rehanging the exhibit items. The importance of having photographs and renderings, as well as the models, was demonstrated during the visit of President Theodore Roosevelt and his cabinet to the exhibition hall. When Roosevelt called the models of the Washington Monument gardens "fussy," Senator McMillan immediately rushed him over to the large renderings of the plan prepared by Jules Guerin and Charles Graham. Roosevelt, it is said, then became "enthusiastic" about the Park Commission plans.

Rejected Plans

In addition to the plans approved for Washington—those, for example, of L'Enfant, Downing, and the Senate Park Commission—many other plans have been proposed but rejected. A sampling of some of the plans presented to the Congress for consideration follows:

1) In 1797, Nicholas King, surveyor of the City of Washington, prepared for the city's board of commissioners his Wharfing Plans for the orderly development of Washington's waterfront. Only a portion of his proposal was ever carried into effect.

2) In 1816, Benjamin Latrobe, surveyor of the City of Washington, presented a plan for a university in the capital city (figure 45). The idea of creating such a university was a dream cherished by George Washington. Latrobe's plan is similar to the plan adopted for the University of Virginia, founded in 1817 by Thomas Jefferson. In both plans, connected wings (or "ranges") to house professors and students flanked an axis extending from a central library (and also, in Latrobe's design, an observatory). Jefferson and Latrobe worked closely together and it is difficult to determine whose influence was predominant in the design.

3) In 1841, Robert Mills, architect of public buildings, presented a plan for

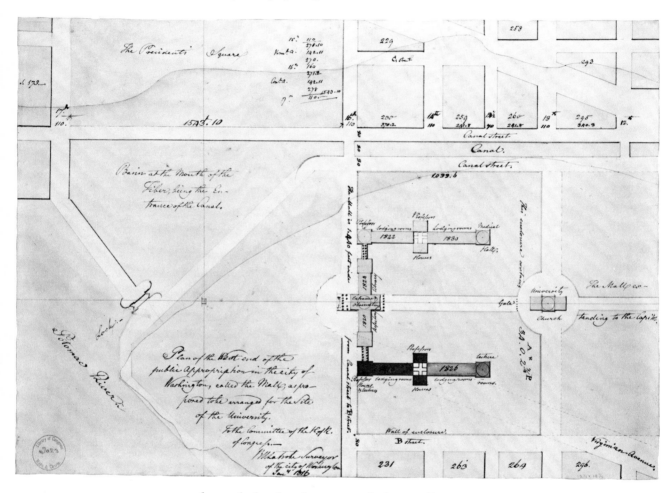

the orderly development of the Mall, particularly in the area between Seventh and Twelfth Streets, NW. Mills's plan was prepared during the debate over how the Smithsonian Institution should be organized.

4) In 1901, George Keller, an architect of Hartford, Connecticut, proposed balancing the Washington Monument with an identical obelisk dedicated to Abraham Lincoln (figure 46). Keller pointed out that by the ancient Egyptians, obelisks were "usually erected in pairs as memorials to their great dead, one on either side of the gates of the temples." He rejected the Park Commission's attempt to balance the Washington Monument by a series of sunken gardens, or any other attempted solution that ignored the disparity in height between the monument and whatever sought to balance it.

LOST WASHINGTON: Should we automatically preserve our existing architectural heritage? The answer is not simple. Buildings deteriorate, their original purposes often superseded. Population pressures, tax laws, real estate

FIGURE 46. *Watercolor Sketch of Washington by George Keller, 1901. This painting by George Keller, of Hartford, Connecticut, shows two identical obelisks. The caption for the work is "Scheme for location of Memorial Bridge and Monuments: Grouping of Public Buildings and Improvement of the Mall, Washington, D.C."*

Courtesy American Antiquarian Society, Worcester, Massachusetts.

FIGURE 47. Prisoners to a Grid, *drawing by Nancy Wolf, 1973. Charcoal on paper, mylar, and metalized mylar.*

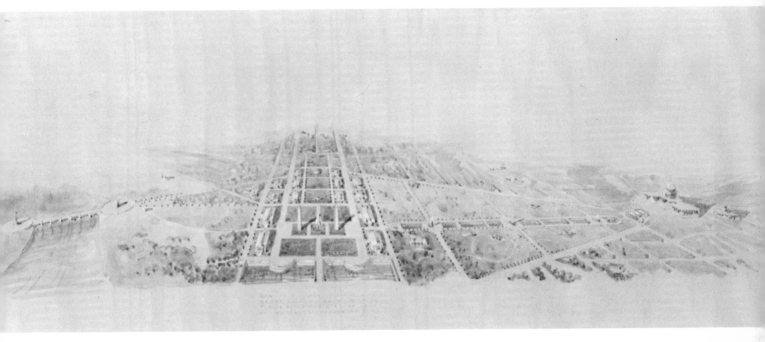

values, changing fashions often make it difficult to preserve even the best buildings of the past. The values—good or bad—of the future must be weighed against the values—good or bad—of the past. Bad buildings may replace good ones; good ones may replace bad ones. Preservationists have sensitized builders to the possibility that restoration of old structures for new uses can sometimes be good business. Planners now seek to incorporate the best of the past in their plans for the future (figures 47, 48, 49).

Current Plans

The unprecedented growth of the Washington metropolitan area in the 1950s and 1960s stimulated the federal government to plan and direct that growth. In 1952, Congress restructured the National Capital Planning Commission as the central planning agency for the federal and District governments. In 1961, the NCPC and its regional collaborator, the National Capital Regional Planning Council—since succeeded in part by the Metropolitan Washington Council of Governments—issued "A Policies Plan for the Year 2000: The Nation's Capital." The underlying assumptions of the planning for Washington in the second half of the twentieth century have been:

1) the expectation of continued and rapid growth in the national capital region beyond the original limits of the District of Columbia; *2)* the need to

FIGURE 48. *Convention Hall Market, 1928. The Northern Liberty Market, Fifth and K Streets, NW, was built in 1874 to replace the older market, at Mount Vernon Square, demolished in 1872. Designed by the prominent Washington architect, James H. McGill, the new Northern Liberty Market, at the time of its construction, had the largest unsupported roof span in the country. The interior consisted of one immense room which accommodated 284 vendor stalls. In 1891, a second floor was added to serve as* an auditorium and the name of building was changed to Convention Hall Market. When the Center Market, located at Eighth Street and Pennsylvania Avenue, NW, was demolished in 1932, the vendors moved to the Convention Hall Market and renamed it Center Market. In subsequent years, the building housed a wax museum. It is now deserted, and of the original construction, only the outer walls remain. Courtesy **Washington Star** and National Geographic Society.*

direct this growth along transportation corridors radiating from the central city; and 3) the need to maintain open space between the corridors of growth (figure 26).

President John F. Kennedy, in a memorandum dated 27 November 1962, for the heads of executive departments and establishments and the commissioners of the District of Columbia, adopted the corridor cities concept recommended by the Year 2000 Plan and ordered all agencies of the executive branch to plan their future operations with a view to its implementation. President Kennedy's memorandum also directed the planning of new public offices in "nonmonumental buildings" to be located in "relatively small but strategically situated groups in and adjacent to the Central Business District." Kennedy's memorandum represented a move away from the formality of the Senate Park Commission planners of 1901 and back toward the L'Enfant conception of an integral mix of commercial and government functions.

The fierce debate between partisans of the automobile highway transportation system necessary to support the Year 2000 Plan and advocates of a

rapid rail transit system was waged during the 1950s and 1960s. Both sides presently agree that a "balanced" or "coordinated" system of transportation is necessary, though the details of this mix are still subject to debate. The construction of the Capital Beltway during the 1960s created a new automobile-oriented "core" for the metropolitan area, linked to the older federal and residential city by automobile-dominated commuter arterials. The construction of the Metro rail system in the 1970s is expected to enhance the 1961 radial corridor concept by providing more viable links between the newer regional city on the periphery and the older federal and residential core. The National Capital Planning Commission's comprehensive planning approach gradually shifted in the 1960s from a primary emphasis upon the whole city in its regional setting to a greater consideration of smaller units (communities, neighborhoods) within the metropolitan area. The planning on both levels is expressed in a continually revised Comprehensive Plan for the National Capital.

THE PENNSYLVANIA AVENUE REDEVELOPMENT SCHEME: The shabby condition of the north side of Pennsylvania Avenue—as viewed on the inaugural ride to the Capitol in 1961—caused President John F. Kennedy to initiate plans, soon after his inauguration, to rebuild the avenue. The south side of the avenue was defined by vaguely classical and carefully coordinated office buildings constructed between 1929 and 1938 as part of the Federal Triangle project. This project had eliminated a mass of deteriorated nineteenth-century commercial and residential buildings, many of which had important historic associations. The north side of the avenue has remained a mixture of many small decaying Victorian commercial buildings interspersed with a few large-scale but undistinguished office buildings. The avenue planners, led by Nathaniel Owings, sought to match the south side with a north side of equivalent dignity but greater humanity. The planners were aware of the danger of creating walled canyons of government buildings occupied only during the daylight hours of weekdays. They sought instead to create a mix of government buildings, commercial establishments, and residential structures in order to bring life to the area both night and day, weekdays and weekends.

The initial proposal for redeveloping Pennsylvania Avenue called for a wide setback on the north side of the avenue, removal of buildings projecting ahead of the new line, and the creation of a large "National Square" in the area at the junction of Pennsylvania Avenue and the White House grounds. In the process of public debate and official review, major modifications have been made to the plan (see figure 29). Principal among these modifications has been the diminution in the size of the open space at the Fifteenth Street, NW, terminus of the avenue to the dimensions shown on the model (allowing the retention of the old Willard Hotel—figure 14—and the block on which it stands), and the acceptance of a projection beyond the new street line of several buildings of architectural merit, such as the National Bank of Washington and Apex Liquors. Although planning policy recently formulated would retain the old Post Office, debate still continues on whether to renovate, restore, or demolish part of the building in order to complete the great plaza of the Federal Triangle.

THE STORY OF THE EIGHTH STREET HOUSING COMPLEX: This work of Washington architect Hugh Newell Jacobsen and the designers of the Pennsylvania Avenue Development Corporation is an imaginative solution to the problem of creating a mix of housing, shops, and offices in the heart of Washington. The plan shows how housing can have high density and still be varied, and how automobiles can be retained yet subordinated to the requirements of city living. The principal problem faced by a residential project in the central city is the high ground rent which must somehow be absorbed. In this case, the corporation has suggested that a major portion of the ground rent can be absorbed by creating underground storage for the National Archives beneath the site. The over-all plan for the avenue's redevelopment has been approved by Congress and awaits funding. Certain elements of the housing design are still at issue with the National Capital Planning Commission, which is concerned both with the narrowing of the visual axis down Eighth Street, NW, and with funding.

SECTIONAL DIVISIONS AND RIVALRY IN THE DISTRICT OF COLUMBIA: Washington's street system is divided into four quadrants centered on the Capitol Building:

Northeast Quadrant. Streets east of North Capitol Street and north of East Capitol Street.

Southeast Quadrant. Streets south of East Capitol Street and east of South Capitol Street.

Northwest Quadrant. Streets north of the Mall (which takes the place of a nonexistent West Capitol Street) and west of North Capitol Street.

Southwest Quadrant. Streets south of the Mall and west of South Capitol Street.

Visitors to Washington at the right street address often find themselves in the wrong quadrant, since the lettered streets are the same on both sides of the east-west dividing line and the numbered streets are the same on both sides of the north-south dividing line.

Residents of the eastern portion of the District of Columbia have persistently charged that residents of the western portion have been favored over them. Jefferson expected that Washington's commercial heart would be along the Eastern Branch (Anacostia River). In fact, however, the eastern portion of the District never achieved commercial or political prominence. Why? Reasons often given have included the greater attractiveness of the western quarters of the District, the more certain water supply piped in from the West, the prevailing westerly winds, the higher (more healthy) ground, and the like. Many residents of the eastern districts, on the other hand, have disagreed with such explanations and asserted that the self-interest of District government officials residing in the northwest quadrant consciously or unconsciously inclined them to favor more improvements in their area than elsewhere.

Who's in Charge Here?

Responsibility for planning the development of Washington is diffused rather than concentrated.

THE NATIONAL CAPITAL PLANNING COMMISSION: Created by Congress in 1924 as the National Capital Park Commission, this agency became in 1926 the National Capital Park and Planning Commission. In 1952 it was restructured by Congress and renamed the National Capital Planning Commission. Its purpose was to serve as the "central planning agency for the Federal and District governments to plan the appropriate and orderly development and redevelopment of the National Capital. . . ." Since the 1974 District of Columbia Home Rule Act, the NCPC serves as the central *federal* planning agency for the development and redevelopment of the National Capital. The commission reviews local plans prepared by the District government to determine their impact on the federal establishment. The commission also is responsible for preservation of important natural and historic features of the National Capital.

THE PENNSYLVANIA AVENUE DEVELOPMENT CORPORATION: The Pennsylvania Avenue Development Corporation is responsible for the improvement of the major ceremonial axis between the White House and the Capitol along the north side of Pennsylvania Avenue, though its recommendations touch on the redevelopment of the Mall and changes on the south side of Pennsylvania Avenue. The corporation is the successor to the Pennsylvania Avenue Advisory Council, which was created by President Kennedy in 1962 and had as its first chairman architect Nathaniel A. Owings of California.

THE COMMISSION OF FINE ARTS: The Commission of Fine Arts gives special attention to aesthetic problems affecting the development of the capital, more particularly concerning the design and location of public buildings, statues, and monuments. Established in 1910, before the creation of any permanent planning body in the nation's capital, the commission was instrumental in persuading Congress to follow through on the Senate Park Commission's recommendations to extend the Mall west and to build the Lincoln Memorial and the Memorial Bridge. The commission's "watchdog of appearance" role is understood and respected by all.

THE NATIONAL PARK SERVICE: The National Park Service, a branch of the Department of Interior, has special responsibility for the Mall and related park areas of Washington. While concerned primarily with maintaining the parks system, the National Park Service can initiate and influence the planning of changes and additions to the park areas within the regions under National Park Service jurisdiction.

FIGURE 50. The Urban Planners, *drawing by*
Nancy Wolf, 1973. Pencil on paper.

THE DISTRICT OF COLUMBIA: The government of the District of Columbia
is charged with various responsibilities including building and fire regulations, zoning, and police protection. Since the coming of home rule, it has
taken over local planning and is responsible for planning functions for nonfederal portions of the city, functions formerly exercised by the National
Capital Planning Commission.

ELEMENTS OF PLANNING

Planners, from L'Enfant to the National Capital Planning Commission, have defined in various ways the elements in the comprehensive process by which the city has been shaped to its present form. For example, L'Enfant spoke of a "reciprocity of sight" along the "lines" or "avenues" between his squares and circles. The architectural historian Kevin Lynch emphasizes the importance of "nodes," strategic points where paths cross or meet in cities. And the National Capital Planning Commission has expanded on the vocabulary of planning terms, as indicated in its "Proposed Urban Design Concepts" map of 1972.

The Federal City Exhibition separates the planning elements, as applied to Washington, into the following categories: suburbs, alleys, public buildings (federal offices, District markets, District schools and libraries), educational institutions, bridges, circles, water, trees, vistas, transportation (airports, railroads, Metro, parkways, streets and highways), and parks.

Suburbs

Why did they mushroom? The migration of the well-to-do from the center city to the suburbs was unstoppable when new means of transportation (the trolley, the automobile) made such movement easy. Fresh air, grassy lawns, physical safety, congenial neighbors, easy access: all these advantages—glowingly proclaimed in advertisements even before the turn of the century (figure 51)—were eagerly seized by Washingtonians in a movement that continues unabated to this day. Increasingly, however, the advantages of the suburbs are lost by virtue of the very numbers engaged in the search. Fresh air, physical safety, easy access: all are reduced in proportion to the numbers seeking them. The massive "developments" on the periphery of Washington (figures 23, 24) illustrate this chaotic and frustrating effort to combine urban and rural values.

Alleys

Alley dwellings (figure 52) to house the poor began to be built on a limited scale in Washington prior to the Civil War. At first the great majority of alley dwellers were white. After the war, as population swelled, alley dwellers increased in numbers, the vast majority being black. In 1892, alarmed by the existence of crime and disease in enclaves in the heart of the city, Congress ordered alley construction halted. At the same time, the introduction of trolleys (and later automobiles) relieved the pressure on intown housing, since the alley was to some degree the product of a pedestrian city. The City

FIGURE 51. *"Palisades of the Potomac," 1890. This colored lithograph advertises the Palisades of the Potomac as having "scenery unsurpassed." The ad also mentions "salubrity and health unquestioned; pure air and pure water . . . ." The inscription at the bottom right reads, "The most picturesque portion of the District of Columbia and destined to shortly become the most fashionable as well as the most desirable suburb of Washington." Lithograph copyright by Jacob Clark and E. B. Cottrell.*

Courtesy American Antiquarian Society, Worcester, Massachusetts.

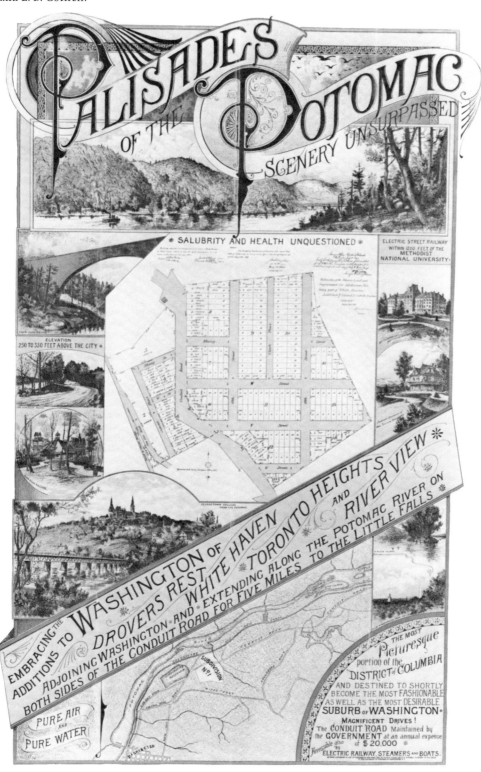

101

FIGURE 52. *Purdy's Court, 1908. This back alley was near the Capitol grounds in Washington.*

Photograph by Lewis Wickes Hine, courtesy International Museum of Photography at George Eastman House, Rochester, New York.

Beautiful movement, emphasizing order and separation of functions, provided further reasons for eliminating the more constricted alley dwellings. In the 1960s, there was movement by the well-to-do back into the city and the beginnings of restoration activity in the central city. During this period, the few remaining alley dwellings obtained a new lease on life. Once synonymous with crime, some now became quite fashionable. As the pedestrian city revives, urban planners have taken another look at alley dwellings. Like the "housegroups" recommended by C. A. Doxiadis, the alley provides controlled access and "defensible space" for a large group of residences, and encourages neighborliness and cooperation among the inhabitants.

Public Buildings

Most of Washington's important buildings are designed to house the public functions of the federal government, and to serve the private needs of its employees. From an aesthetic point of view, Washington is an open air museum reflecting the changing tastes of the American people.

FEDERAL OFFICES: The earliest and still predominant federal style is the classical. Thomas Jefferson, who was explicit in his admiration for classical architecture, is usually credited with turning American taste in this direction. By mid-twentieth century the classical form was still respected, but hardly recognizable in the attenuated form reached in buildings such as the House of Representatives' Rayburn Office Building and the Smithsonian Institution's National Museum of History and Technology.

While the first half of the nineteenth century was dominated by classical buildings such as the Patent Office Building, the second half of the century saw the emergence of a variety of styles such as Italian Renaissance (the Pension Building) and French Second Empire (the State, War and Navy Building). The twentieth century has produced more massive and utilitarian buildings, such as those built in the Federal Triangle in the 1930s (figure 53), the Pentagon (hastily constructed at the outset of World War II), and executive agency buildings constructed in the 1960s on the south side of Independence Avenue to meet the skyrocketing demand for federal office space.

THE PATENT OFFICE BUILDING: The Patent Office Building at Eighth and F Streets, NW, reflects the tendency of Americans in the early years of the republic to search for models of future greatness in ancient Greece and Rome. This building was built between 1838 and 1867 and is now a part of the Smithsonian Institution. Its exterior is frankly derivative from classical Greek temple forms. Although the façade was almost literally ordered out of a copybook, the interior contains beautiful and functional rooms designed in varying historical styles and utilizing various technological innovations, the product of its several architects, from Robert Mills to Edward Clark.

THE PENSION BUILDING: The Pension Building, completed in 1883, was designed by the military engineer, Montgomery Meigs, to house the clerks required to handle the pensions of Civil War veterans. Meigs's "Old Red Barn," as it was sarcastically referred to, is essentially a giant envelope of space providing maximum work area (on the main floor and around the galleries) at minimum cost in an era before efficient artificial lighting and air conditioning. Its outer form reflects the influence of the Palazzo Farnese. The frieze that encircles the building, reminiscent of that encircling the Parthenon, depicts the activities of the victorious Union army.

THE STATE, WAR AND NAVY BUILDING: Alfred B. Mullett's State, War and Navy Building, built in 1871–88 in the French Second Empire style much admired in its day, now houses executive offices of the president (figure 54). Its appearance fell out of fashion soon after the building was completed, and it has been the subject of a number of proposed face-liftings. Fortunately the building was not rebuilt in the classical style to match the Treasury Department on the east side of the White House.

District Markets

Farmers' markets were a part of the early plans for Washington. Markets (figure 48) were established in the city's western, northern, central, and eastern areas. The Eastern Market (figure 55) is still used as such a market. Formerly, farmers came in by farm wagon or handcart to sell their products. Now they truck their products to market and have been joined by entrepreneurs bringing commodities produced at distant points and purchased through middlemen. Outside the market, food is sold directly from trucks. Inside, specialized shops sell cheese, meats, fruits, bread, and other foods. The market provides an opportunity for ethnic diversity in the sale and purchase of foodstuffs. This ethnic diversity usually is absent in supermarkets, which increasingly are finding the central city economically unsuitable to their operations. The give and take of verbal exchange with individually known merchants, the pleasure of meeting neighbors and acquaintances, the healthy character of a walk to and from the market—all are values that have impressed the city authorities under whose jurisdiction the farmers' markets are maintained. The Eastern Market, now in the center of a thriving restoration area, is being refurbished to extend its life as a market.

FIGURE 56. *Franklin School, ca. 1900. This building is located at the southeast corner of Thirteenth and K Streets, NW.*

Photograph by Frances Benjamin Johnston, courtesy Library of Congress.

District Schools and Libraries

Another function of government is the building of schools for the education of the citizens of the District of Columbia. Washington's school architecture has been of a high quality as shown by the Franklin School (figure 56), still standing though no longer used as a school, and by many modern schools.

The District of Columbia Martin Luther King Memorial Library, designed by Ludwig Mies van der Rohe, is the famous Chicago architect's only building in Washington. Its restrained, understated lines, its rejection of ornament and celebration of function, make it one of Washington's finest examples of contemporary American architecture.

Educational Institutions

Washington's institutions of higher education have developed comprehensive planning within limited areas of the city. The George Washington University, Georgetown University, The Catholic University of America, and Howard University are perhaps the best-known institutions of higher education within the District. There are others which should not be overlooked.

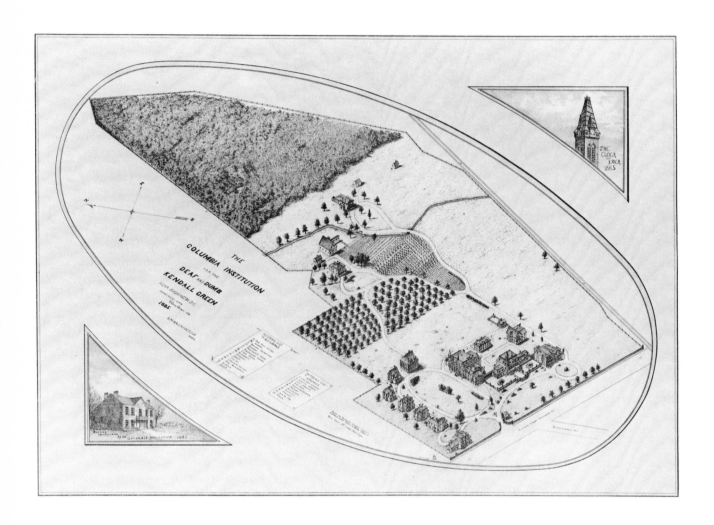

GALLAUDET COLLEGE: The Columbia Institution for the Deaf and Dumb, incorporated in 1857, was renamed Gallaudet College in 1894 in honor of Thomas Hopkins Gallaudet, founder of education for the deaf in America. Gallaudet College occupies a site in northeast Washington known as Kendall Green after Amos Kendall, founder of the school. In the words of Edward Miner Gallaudet, son of Thomas Hopkins Gallaudet and president of the college from 1864 to 1911, the Gallaudet site beyond Florida Avenue was "unspeakably ugly—more like a great stockyard than any thing else I can think of." After the school came under the wing of Congress, the expanding campus began to assume a more pleasing aspect, as is evident in the site sketch drawn in 1885 by Glenn Brown (figure 57). Most of the structures pictured in Brown's sketch continue to stand and serve their original purpose.

THE ARMY WAR COLLEGE: The Army War College (now called the National War College) was founded in 1901 and occupies a partially reclaimed riverfront site at Fort McNair in the Southwest, along with the Industrial College of the Armed Forces and the Inter-American Defense College. The War College, originally proposed by Secretary of War Elihu Root in 1899, was established in 1901. The present layout and main building was begun in 1903 and completed in 1907. The design was conceived by the architectural firm of McKim, Mead and White, and executed by Captain John S. Sewell of the Army Corps of Engineers.

Charles McKim, member of the Senate Park Commission, had been lunching with Senator McMillan and Secretary of War Root one day and was shown proposed plans for the barracks. The barracks were to be on the south end of the site looking down the Potomac towards Mount Vernon while the main building and officers' houses were located on the north end adjacent to the carbarns. McKim recommended that the two locations be reversed, that the houses for the officers be located along the river and be designed with broad piazzas with white columns fronting the parade ground. "Then you will have a regiment on parade!" he noted. Secretary of War Root was impressed and insisted then that McKim's firm build the War College.

The ground was unstable, however, so many of the structures had to be placed over concrete pilings. Several buildings in the center of the post blocked the vista of the completed War College from the flagpole area, but were not torn down—in violation of McKim's plan—on plea that the housing shortage made razing them inadvisable. This failure by the army to carry out the agreed-upon design so offended Stanford White, architectural partner of McKim, that on a visit to the site he abruptly turned his carriage around and left without visiting the building designed by his firm (figure 58).

AMERICAN UNIVERSITY: The campus for the American University, created by the Methodist Church of the United States, was designed in 1893 by the landscape architecture firm of the Olmsteds, already famous for their participation in the design of the federal city. The present campus at Nebraska and Massachusetts Avenues, NW, has not followed the Olmsteds' plan in specific detail but in over-all layout still reflects the original design.

Bridges

MEMORIAL BRIDGE: A bridge over the Potomac "symbolical of the firmly established Union of the North and the South" was proposed by Daniel Webster in 1851. By the end of the century, plans had matured for such a bridge connecting Washington and Arlington Memorial Cemetery in Virginia. The specific location and design of the bridge were determined by the Senate Park Commission of 1901. As the secretary of the commission, Charles Moore, put it in a later memoir, "On the steps of the little temple at the Villa Borghese [in Rome, where the commission members had stopped on their 1901 tour of Europe] the determination was reached that the Memorial Bridge be a low structure on a line from the site of the Lincoln Memorial [another proposal of the commission] to the Arlington Mansion—a monumental rather than a traffic bridge, but a significant element in an extensive

park scheme." This vision was a long time in its realization. The final design, by McKim, Mead and White, was not accepted by Congress until 1924. The Memorial Bridge is a deceptively simple and graceful structure. Actually, it is a drawbridge which contains elaborate machinery—virtually invisible under the roadway—for opening the heavy center section. This drawbridge section has not been used in recent years.

THEODORE ROOSEVELT BRIDGE: In contrast to the consciously symbolic Memorial Bridge, the neighboring Theodore Roosevelt Bridge (figure 59) is purely functional. Opened in 1964, this bridge expresses the technology of highway builders in the service of commuters seeking automobile access from suburbia to downtown employment. At one point, rather than to pro-

111

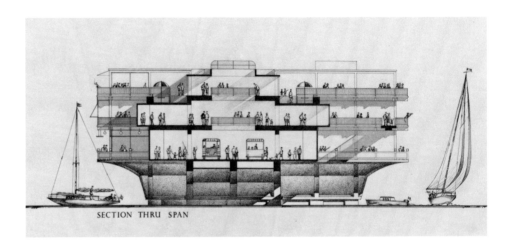

SECTION THRU SPAN

vide a bridge, some planners hoped to tunnel under the Potomac to Virginia, but high costs discouraged this approach—and the bridge was built. In the words of Julian Eugene Kulski, "the Roosevelt Bridge is neither a bridge, nor a highway, nor a piece of sculpture." Multiple access and exit ramps emphasize its utilitarian, nonaesthetic, and nonsymbolic functions.

PROPOSED WASHINGTON CHANNEL BRIDGE: In 1966 Washington architect Chloethiel Woodard Smith proposed a bridge connecting the waterfront area of the Southwest with East Potomac Park. The bridge would contain a multitude of shops and restaurants overlooking an enlarged marina on both sides of the Washington Channel (figure 60). The rental income from these establishments was expected to pay for the bridge. The bridge would provide access for pedestrians who could also utilize a special mass transportation vehicle running through the insides of the bridge. At present, the only access between East Potomac Park and the Southwest is the Channel Crossing Bridge of the Southwest Freeway, and by a circuitous route under the Fourteenth Street Bridge.

Circles

It has often been asserted that Washington's street system, particularly its circles, were designed to facilitate military defense against both domestic insurrection and foreign invasion. Artillery placed in the numerous circles, so the theory runs, could clear the radiating streets of any accumulated rabble. Though plausible, the theory lacks supporting evidence. It is true that defense against foreign invasion of the city was contemplated. Such attacks,

FIGURE 61. *Logan Circle, October 1950. This aerial view shows the circle at the crossing of Thirteenth Street and Rhode Island and Vermont Avenues, NW.*
Washington Star *photograph.*

however, if they were to occur, were anticipated from the sea; forts to defend against such attacks were constructed on the water approaches to Washington. Possible domestic disturbances, which might interfere with the orderly functioning of Congress, were to be countered by militia and regular forces stationed in the capital. Washington's circles (figure 61), like its squares, were designed by L'Enfant to provide visual and physical reference points in the urban landscape and serve as centers of the proposed neighborhoods he hoped to develop throughout the city.

Water

The City of Washington was carefully planned to take economic and aesthetic advantage of its site at the place where the tidal waters of the Chesapeake Bay meet the fresh water flowing down from the piedmont. L'Enfant's major axes, both west from the Capitol and south from the President's House, assumed that the eye should look to the river—and to the Virginia hills beyond. L'Enfant provided another dramatic vista at Twelfth Street, SW, looking down the Potomac toward Mount Vernon. This vista was eliminated, however, in the redrawing of L'Enfant's plan by Andrew Ellicott (figure 2). Other connections to water, including a continuous waterfront street, were planned, but few were developed.

Two rivers, the Potomac and the Anacostia, formed the principal "arms" within which the new city was cradled. Tiber Creek penetrated into the heart of the federal District and was lovingly exploited by both L'Enfant and Andrew Jackson Downing as the site of a canal connecting the two rivers. L'Enfant proposed to have a cascade of water tumbling down Capitol Hill into the canal. These watercourses envisioned by L'Enfant—suggestive of the canals of Venice—would, he anticipated, be "beautiful above what can be imagined."

Although the cascade from the Capitol was never built, the Washington Canal (figure 35) was. Designed to connect with the Chesapeake & Ohio Canal's (figure 62) Georgetown segment at the present Seventeenth Street, NW, the city canal ran east along what is now Constitution Avenue and eventually turned southeast, west of the Capitol along the present Canal Street. Unhappily, by Andrew Jackson Downing's time, in 1851, the Washington Canal had degenerated into an eyesore; it had become an open sewer (figure 9). Downing proposed revitalizing the canal; along it, according to Downing's conception, sailing craft would move under elegant bridges. Today, the canal has been replaced by cement, but Tiber Creek continues to

114

FIGURE 62. *Traffic on the Chesapeake & Ohio Canal, ca. 1910.*
Photograph from the Proctor Collection, courtesy Columbia Historical Society.

flow beneath Constitution Avenue through two immense tunnels big enough for streetcars! In another carry-over from the past, the southwest quadrant of the city is sometimes called Tiber Island, reminiscent of the days when this area was literally separated from the rest of the city by the canal.

Over the years, Washington planners have dotted the urban landscape with fountains and pools. The cooling effect of water is frequently cited as a principal justification. In fact, a shallow pool of water set in masonry and without dense, nearby trees is no cooler in the hot summer than the surrounding pavement, whereas good shade trees can reduce temperatures several degrees lower than grass or water that is unshaded by trees.

Trees

Washington is a city of trees. When entering the District from the suburbs, the traveler is immediately aware of the geographical distinction as he passes through the rich border of trees along Washington's streets. Thomas Jefferson had worked out a complex scheme for planting poplars and other trees along Pennsylvania Avenue (see figure 80). Andrew Jackson Downing in the 1850s proved that evergreens would flourish in Washington's southern climate. Mayor (or "Boss") Alexander Shepherd, after the Civil War, was responsible for the most concentrated planting effort in Washington's history.

The effect of trees is to soften the rigid outlines of roads and buildings and, by gracefully growing together in a natural arch, to unify the two sides of the street. Trees help to link the ends of avenues by the leafy tunnel they create along the axes (figure 63). Trees humanize the streets by providing shade and coolness in summer, protection against the wind as well as aesthetic relief in winter. The lavish use of trees by Downing on the Mall and by Frederick Law Olmsted, Sr., on the Capitol grounds contrasts sharply with the formal treatments sought for those areas by Pierre L'Enfant or the Senate Park Commission. The dialogue between advocates of the formal versus informal approach to city planning continues to this day.

Vistas

L'Enfant designed Washington as a city of vistas. The axis from the Capitol to the Washington Monument, one of L'Enfant's original and principal vistas, still remains today. Others of the L'Enfant vistas have been blocked by carelessness, and some even by design.

THE EIGHTH STREET AXIS: One of the principal cross axes planned by L'Enfant ran south to the shores of the Potomac from a point north of the proposed National Church or Pantheon, in actuality the site at Eighth and F Streets, NW, on which was built the Patent Office (now the National Portrait Gallery and the National Collection of Fine Arts). This axis was not like the broad open avenue (now the Mall) L'Enfant had designed as the major east-west axis (see figure 1). It was a *narrow* axis, centered on Eighth Street and punctuated periodically by broad squares, or monumental buildings, extending between Seventh and Ninth Streets. The rhythm of the "stops" in this axis has been altered in recent years by the addition of the National Archives Building north of the Mall and the Government Services Administration Building south of it. Yet, Eighth Street remains an axis for north-south movement. The circular Hirshhorn Museum on the south edge of the Mall encourages the eye to move around it north and south. The Sculpture Garden of the Hirshhorn Museum originally was planned to run in a north-south direction across the *center* of the Mall. In deference to the feeling of some that the Mall as principal east-west axis should be undisturbed, the Sculpture Garden was realigned to be parallel to that axis rather than cross it.

PENNSYLVANIA AVENUE: Originally, Pennsylvania Avenue was intended to provide a major vista from the Capitol to the White House. When the Treasury Building was erected at the intersection of Pennsylvania Avenue

117

and Fifteenth Street, NW, it caused the most famous (or infamous) blockage of a L'Enfant vista (figure 29). Whether the White House was imposing enough to anchor its end of the avenue without the intervening mass of the Treasury Building is a much-debated subject among planners. Both Downing and Nathaniel Owings sought to redefine the terminus of the axis at the White House end. The erection of the State, War and Navy Building (now the Executive Office Building, figure 54) southwest of the White House similarly cut off another vista running from lower New York Avenue to the White House. The White House nevertheless remains the focal point for numerous vistas, with the Sixteenth Street vista north from the White House being perhaps the most dramatic.

NORTH CAPITOL STREET: The view of the Capitol seen through a swath cut through trees on the grounds of the Soldiers' Home at North Capitol Street is depicted in a photograph from the early twentieth century (figure 64). The rural quality of this view conveys the aspect of remoteness the area possessed when Abraham Lincoln used the Soldiers' Home as an occasional retreat from the oppressive heat of Washington's summers.

TENTH STREET, SOUTHWEST: The possibility of creating a dramatic vista of the rust-colored, towered Smithsonian Institution Building from L'Enfant

119

Plaza in the new Southwest was lost when the Forrestal Building was bridged over Tenth Street at its intersection with Independence Avenue, SW. Planners were divided on the question of emphasizing the north-south Tenth Street axis by leaving the view to the Smithsonian open, or of emphasizing the east-west Independence Avenue axis by carrying the Forrestal Building over Tenth Street. The decision was made to bridge Tenth Street. The view as it would have looked had the vista remained open is shown in figure 65.

Transportation

Transportation routes are the arteries of a great city, and easy circulation is vital to the city's health. No element of planning is more vigorously debated than the form in which a city's transportation arteries should be shaped. Adapting new technologies to a city's transportation needs sometimes involves trade-offs between more efficient movement and a diminished quality of other elements of urban life.

NATIONAL AIRPORT: The present Washington National Airport was built in the mud flats of the Potomac at the beginning of World War II. It provides the most dramatic entrance into Washington from the air. The glide path in, and the take-off path out, pass over the river, which separates the airport from the monumental heart of Washington. The visitor may get a better view and understanding of the physical layout of Washington before he arrives than after he lands. As he comes in for a landing, the Mall, linking the Capitol and the Washington Monument, guides his eye to the monuments which anchor the city's central core. The Mall recalled to memory is the bird's-eye and postcard-size view perceived from several thousand feet up in the air. Once on the ground at National Airport, the arriving passenger is seized by urban congestion and confusion until he is on the George Washington Memorial Parkway headed north to the city, and then once more the symbolic centers begin to dominate the landscape over the low-profile buildings of the Southwest. With the completion of Washington's Metro system, arriving and departing passengers will be able to go to and from terminals by high-speed rail transportation.

DULLES INTERNATIONAL AIRPORT: Dulles International Airport is thirty miles west of the Capitol in the rolling hills of Virginia and serves international routes and distant cities in the United States. For the visitor arriving at National Airport, clarity reigns in the sky, confusion on the ground. In contrast, the visitor arriving at Dulles International Airport descends from

an unfamiliar sky into a reception center of unequalled clarity and beauty.

Eero Saarinen's airport skillfully separates the functions of take-off and landing, loading and unloading passengers, arriving and leaving the terminal, and storing and recovering one's private transportation. As a result the passenger walks fewer steps in Saarinen's spectacular terminal building than in any other airport in the United States. Technically exciting in its use of a cable-hung curved roof, Saarinen's open terminal at once clarifies the visitor's options, stimulates his eye, and relaxes his mind (figure 66). Unfortunately, the exaltation of the airport is not sustained by the long motor trip

121

to Washington. Future planning undoubtedly will provide a mass transportation link that will relate the airport more intimately and efficiently to the city it is meant to serve.

RAILROADS: Modeled on the Roman Baths of Caracalla, the Union Station (figures 18, 67) is Washington's great monument to the railroad era. The station remains as the single passenger terminal for rail lines entering the city and now serves as a bus terminal and Visitor Center for tourists coming to the Washington area.

Location and design of the station are the result of the vision and energy of Daniel Burnham, who exploited his double role as chairman of the Senate Park Commission and architect for the Pennsylvania Railroad. The railroad, which owned a station and tracks on the Mall in 1900 (figure 39), voluntarily agreed to relocate its terminal on the proposed Union Station site when Burnham begged the president of the railroad to do so as a civic duty. The government facilitated the move by providing land and financial support. As soon as the Union Station opened in 1907, the two railroad stations then serving the city, at Sixth Street, NW, and B Street (now Constitution Avenue) and at New Jersey Avenue and C Street, NW, were immediately demolished.

METRO: Metro—the largest public works project in the history of the United States—is currently making its way under the Washington street plan laid out by L'Enfant.

Though largely invisible, this Metro system of high-speed rail transit will have a revolutionary impact on the city. In effect, Metro (figure 68) will more than double the capacity of existing means of transportation to move people into and out of the city, and it will do so with greater speed and efficiency. Metro was the result of laboriously worked out agreements among the District of Columbia, the states of Virginia and Maryland, and the federal government. Its impact is being felt even in advance of any formal opening. Two expected results of the system are more intensive commercial and residential density in areas adjacent to stations, and a stemming of the rising level of pollution caused by automobile exhaust in the city. Washington's fleet of motor buses will become auxiliaries to the rail transit core, "feeding" into Metro terminals from the outlying suburbs.

PARKWAYS: A drive down the George Washington Memorial Parkway on the Virginia side of the Potomac demonstrates that access to the city by road can be exhilarating as well as expeditious. The first survey for such a road from Washington to Mount Vernon was made by Engineer Lieutenant Colonel Peter C. Hains in 1889 in response to a congressional directive. Hains

FIGURE 67. *Union Station Lobby, ca. 1908.*
Courtesy Library of Congress.

proposed a road having the character of a "monumental structure" which would treat both the natural and historical character of the area with reverence. Authorization for the highway finally was voted in 1928 as part of the 1932 bicentennial celebration of George Washington's birth. The George Washington Parkway winds sinuously along the sluggish tidal inlets below the fall line and, carefully hugging the precipitous slope of the river bank, makes its way above the City of Washington to its present junction with the Capital Beltway near the Great Falls of the Potomac.

FIGURE 68. *Metro Station and New Subway Cars, June 1975.*

Courtesy Washington Metropolitan Area Transit Authority.

The parkway provides visual relief in its tie to the landscape as well as visual stimulation in its views of the Capitol, the Washington Monument, and other elements of the nation's capital. It remains today one of the most beautiful urban parkways in the nation. In 1975, a bicycle path paralleling the George Washington Parkway was completed from Washington to Mount Vernon. The path provides opportunities for commuting to the city as well as for recreation along the river.

STREETS AND HIGHWAYS: City planner Lewis Mumford has charged that L'Enfant allocated an excessive amount of space in his plan to streets and highways as opposed to space for public buildings, grounds, and reservations. Until the 1960s, Washington's street system seemed capable of meeting the demands of the automobile and its millions of owners who filled up the growing suburban fringes of the nation's capital in the twentieth century. But even L'Enfant's broad avenues (figure 12) could not accommodate the technology and values of the motor age. Despite the addition of an outer beltway (figure 25) beyond the city's limits and a partial inner loop highway imposed over the generous roadways bequeathed by L'Enfant, the demands of the automobile were ever-expanding, devouring whatever increased access was afforded (figure 69). In the 1970s, planners began to curb automobile access to Washington in the interest of the urban functions being threatened by the escalated automobile traffic.

FIGURE 69. *Morning Rush-Hour Traffic on the Southeast/Southwest Freeway, 13 July 1975. In this view from the southeast toward the Washington Monument, the Lincoln Memorial is seen in the upper left. The round structure at the upper right is the Hirshhorn Museum and Sculpture Garden, completed in 1974. Note how the freeway system is superimposed on the diagonal and grid system inherited from L'Enfant, as is especially evident in the sweep of the freeway across Virginia Avenue, SE and SW.* Washington Post *photograph.*

The Evolution of Washington's Park System

The evolution of Washington's parks has been continuous from the "public walks" contemplated by Jefferson, for the Mall, to an area-wide system serving every recreational need. Historically, Andrew Jackson Downing's plan of 1851 anticipated the growing concern for rural retreats within rapidly growing urban areas. With Downing's premature death the following year the plan was left uncompleted. Later on, in 1866, persistently unhealthy conditions in the swampy Potomac flats and Foggy Bottom areas near the White House led Congress to call for a report on relocating the Executive Mansion. Major Nathaniel Michler of the Army Corps of Engineers, author of the resulting report, urged the advantage of the Rock Creek area as a new location for the President's House. While no action was taken on Michler's report, it helped focus attention on this lovely area of "primeval forests and cultivated fields, its running waters, its rocks clothed with rich ferns and mosses. . . ."

THE ROLE OF THE ARMY CORPS OF ENGINEERS: Responsibility for Washington's public buildings and grounds was transferred in 1867 to the Army Corps of Engineers. During the period when a three-man commission administered the District of Columbia, from 1878 to 1967, one commissioner was required to be an engineer officer. Succeeding engineer officers played vital roles in developing Washington's growing park system.

CIRCLES AND SQUARES: Major Orville Babcock succeeded Michler as superintendent of buildings and grounds in 1871. Major Babcock turned Washington's circles and squares into grassy oases, neatly fenced and filled with trees, fountains, and occasionally a minizoo that might contain deer, owls, prairie dogs, and even an eagle.

POTOMAC PARK: From the Potomac mud flats, the Tidal Basin and both West and East Potomac Park (figure 70) emerged during the period from 1874 to 1913. Much of the design grew out of the Senate Park Commission Plan. This park was the achievement of a series of engineer officers of whom the most notable was Peter Hains. Washington, like other east coast cities, has literally created much of its land area by filling in the surrounding waters, a fact rarely understood by visitors.

ROCK CREEK PARK: The dream of a park in Rock Creek Valley took its first major step toward realization in 1889 when Congress lent the District of Columbia money to acquire land in the area. In 1890, Congress appropriated funds to create a National Zoological Park there, to be administered by the Smithsonian Institution. When the Senate Park Commission put its prestige behind the development of Rock Creek Park as part of a comprehensive park

FIGURE 70. *East Potomac Park, ca. 1925. The Bureau of Printing and Engraving is seen to the left, with the Tidal Basin and the future site of the Thomas Jefferson Memorial to the right.*

Courtesy Commission of Fine Arts.

scheme for Washington, the goal came one step closer. Although serious consideration was given to filling in Rock Creek below Massachusetts Avenue and carrying its waters through an underground culvert, the decision was made to keep the valley open, as both the cheapest and the best alternative. A landscape plan for the zoo and for Rock Creek Park was drawn up by the Olmsted firm. The plan for Rock Creek Park set aside much of the reservation for natural "growth areas" while creating appropriate "use areas" with public facilities at carefully chosen points within the park (figure 70*a*).

ANACOSTIA PARK: The Senate Park Commission threw its weight behind the development of parks along the Anacostia River also. Dredging of the badly silted river bed had begun in 1892 under Lieutenant Colonel Peter C. Hains. The reclamation of the Anacostia flats for park purposes has not been fully achieved although Congress has periodically voted funds to develop the area. Jewels in this eastern chain of parkland are the National Arboretum established by the Department of Agriculture in 1929 and the nearby Aquatic Gardens.

THE MONUMENTAL CORE

Washington's monumental core consists of a gigantic triangle anchored by the Capitol, the Washington Monument, and the White House. This triangle, carefully oriented to the topography of the low-lying basin in which the federal city was built, provides the basis of L'Enfant's design and all subsequent modifications.

The Capitol Building

Capitol Hill, then called Jenkins Hill, was the commanding physical feature chosen by L'Enfant for the site of the "Congress House." L'Enfant saw the hill as "a pedestal waiting for a monument." The original Capitol, designed by William Thornton and consisting of two separate wings, was burned by the British during the War of 1812. Benjamin Latrobe and Charles Bulfinch redesigned the Capitol following the fire. Latrobe's two wings, temporarily joined by an arcaded passageway, were eventually united by Bulfinch as a central section capped by a low dome (figures 71, 72). By 1828, all of the eastern and most of the western grounds of the Capitol were enclosed by fences with gatehouses and gateposts designed by Bulfinch.

The present wings of the Capitol were designed and built by Capitol Architect Thomas U. Walter and Army Engineer Officer Montgomery C. Meigs during the administration of President Millard Fillmore in the 1850s (figure 73) at the same time that Andrew Jackson Downing was redesigning the Mall and the White House grounds (see figures 5, 74). The present cast-iron dome, replacing Bulfinch's earlier dome, was completed during the Civil War at the insistence of President Abraham Lincoln who saw its completion as symbolic of the secure future of the Union (figure 9).

The Capitol Building faces east onto what L'Enfant envisaged as a formal plaza; into it run Pennsylvania Avenue and Maryland Avenue. The Statue of Freedom atop the Capitol looks east, and inaugurations are held on the East Front of the Capitol. As architectural historian Paul Spreiregen points out, however, the Capitol, on its other face, looks west to the land "vaguely realizing westward" up the Potomac and to the mountains where America's nineteenth-century destiny lay (figure 75).

The present Capitol grounds were laid out in 1874 by Frederick Law Olmsted, Sr., in the naturalistic tradition with serpentine paths, heavy foliage, and even a brick-towered grotto. Bulfinch's classical gatehouse and gateposts were removed during the Olmsted renovation to be replaced by more Victorian structures. The present walkways and terraces, begun by Olmsted, were completed in the 1890s. (For Olmsted's 1874 plan, see figure 11.)

FIGURE 73. The United States Capitol, 1858. On this engraving made by J. Steel after an original by T. U. Walter, the caption reads, "North East View of the Capitol at Washington, with the New Extension." The verses below the engraving are these:

Our Nations Capital in all the pride/Of architecture guards Potomacs tide.// On yonder eminence, it proudly stands,/A shrine of Freedom built by Freemens hands.//How oft these Halls have echoed to the tread/Of patriots now numbered with the dead.//

Whose bright examples are looked up to still/ Though brawling demagogues their places fill.//Oh! May our Representatives henceforth//Be generous alike to South and North/ Unheeding him who of "Disunion" prates—/ So shall we ever be United States.

Photograph courtesy Library Company of Philadelphia.

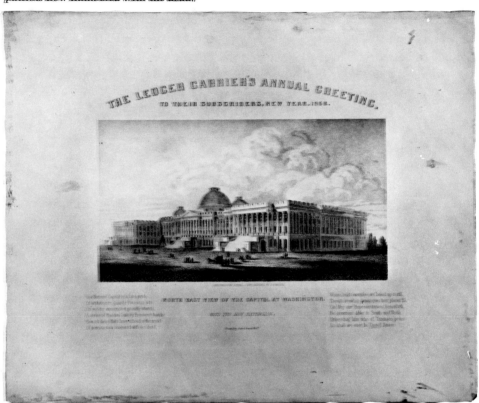

FIGURE 71. The United States Capitol, before 1814. This ink and watercolor sketch, drawn ca. 1819 and attributed to Benjamin Latrobe, shows the Capitol from Pennsylvania Avenue.

Courtesy Library of Congress.

FIGURE 74. *View of the Lincoln Memorial from the Washington Monument, 1975. The rigid lines of the Reflecting Pool evidence the formality of the plans of the Senate Park Commission of 1901. On either side of the Reflecting Pool are contemporary expressions of the informal, naturalistic style of Andrew Jackson Downing's 1851 plan. To the south (to the left of the Reflecting Pool) are the temporary installations of the Smithsonian Institution Festival of American Folklife; to the north (under construction) are the irregularly shaped pools and plantings of Constitution Gardens, designed by Skidmore, Owings and Merrill.*
Photograph by Staples & Charles.

NE

FIGURE 76. Washington Panorama, 1863. This panorama of the Mall and surrounding areas was photographed from the central tower of the Smithsonian Institution Building in 1863 by Titian Ramsay Peale. Notable landmarks are the Washington Monument showing halted construction (in the west [W] view), the Treasury Building (slightly to the right of center in the northwest [NW] view), and the Long Bridge over the Potomac (to the left of center in the southwest [SW] view).

SE

SW

NW

E

Courtesy William Henry Seward Papers, Rush Rhees Library of the University of Rochester.

S

W

N

135

The Mall

The Mall, in Jefferson's original conception of the capital, was to provide a "public walk" in the center of the city linking (less directly than Pennsylvania Avenue) two major foci of the capital, the Congress House and the President's House. L'Enfant provided such a connection, but in the form of an avenue four hundred feet in width and lined with grand residences. L'Enfant's plan was virtually forgotten in the following century though the idea of a public walk linking the two centers of federal power was not. Andrew Jackson Downing provided for such a link in his naturalistic, curvilinear plan of 1851. Although that plan was never fully carried out, the results of Downing's initial plantings and layout of paths are evident in the panorama of the Mall taken by Titian Ramsay Peale in 1863 (figure 76). The canal planned by L'Enfant and restored by Downing—on the site of the present Constitution Avenue—ran under a bridge over Tenth Street, NW, directly north of the Smithsonian tower from which Peale took his pictures. Early complaints of the difficulty of access to the Smithsonian Building from the city led to the construction of this bridge and of a well-drained and well-lighted path across the public grounds to the building.

The Washington Monument

The desire to raise a monument to President George Washington brought forth many conflicting proposals, ranging from simple to complex, from classic to romantic, and from the sublime to the ridiculous. Pierre L'Enfant, in his master plan, proposed that a large statue of Washington on horseback be located at the intersection of the vista running due south from the White House and that running due west from the Capitol at the end of his Grand Avenue (now the Mall).

Congress did nothing specific about erecting a monument to Washington, so a group of private citizens—the Washington National Monument Society —organized a competition for its design in 1833. Robert Mills, the architect, won the competition with a design for a six-hundred-foot obelisk, surrounded at its base by a circular colonnade (figure 77). The monument society approved the obelisk, but not the colonnaded base. Construction on the monument began in 1848. Unfortunately, L'Enfant's proposed site proved to be swampy and unstable. To the dismay of later planners, the Mills-designed monument was begun on a hillock 120 feet *south* and 360 feet *east* of the true axial intersection! By 1856, the private funds donated for the monument's construction ran out, and the half-completed monument stood neglected for twenty years. The change in coloration of the stone is still

FIGURE 77. *Proposed Plan for the Washington National Monument. This watercolor sketch of the Washington National Monument with a colonnaded base was submitted by the architect, Robert Mills, in the design competition organized in 1833.*

Courtesy National Archives.

SKETCH OF

WASHINGTON

NAT!: MONUM!:

BY

ROB!: MILLS,

ARC!.

visible, marking forever where the early construction stopped (figure 78).

In 1876 Congress voted to finish the monument and called for designs for its completion. Competition was spirited. A number of proposals envisaged elaborate Victorian elements built around and concealing the already existing shaft. Other submissions left the uncompleted shaft exposed, but, as proposed by Montgomery C. Meigs, capped it with a figure of a seated Washington under a pillared roof, or, as proposed by C. Seymour Dutton, capped it with a colossal standing statue of Washington exposed to the elements. J. Goldsborough Bruff, a 71-year-old designer, proposed completing the shaft, carrying the height to 501 feet—less than originally proposed, but high enough to gratify the patriotic ambition of those who wished it to be the highest structure in the world. Bruff also provided for two eagle-faced sphinxes to bracket the monument and proposed cutting into the shaft at a level of 100 or 150 feet a liberty cap encircled by the name Washington and the "All-Seeing-Eye of Divine Providence," as it appears in the representation of the Great Seal of the United States on the one-dollar bill. All the proposals eliminated Mills's original plan for the colonnaded pantheon at the base which, as Bruff pointed out, would appear as an "enormous pedestal of one-sixth the entire height of the monument; and the shaft above, seem more like a factory chimney, than a real monument."

The Army Corps of Engineers was given the job of finishing the monument. Noting the perilous condition of the soft sand and clay foundation of the monument, the engineers proposed undergirding it with a thick concrete base. Lieutenant Colonel Thomas Casey was charged with completing the monument, and this he did in 1884. The Washington Monument, in its present simplified form, was dedicated in 1885. When the Senate Park Commission in 1902 presented its elaborate plans for improving the Mall, it faced the problem of the off-center location of the monument. To correct the slight (120 feet) southward deviation, the commission slanted the central grassy strip of the Mall one degree *south* of the true axis. The result is that to the viewer standing on the Mall, the deviation is not at all noticeable, although it is perceptible on maps and from the air. To balance the more serious (360 feet) eastward deviation from the true north-south White House axis, the Park Commission proposed a series of sunken gardens and pools just west of the monument. These gardens and pools were never built because it was found that they would undermine the monument.

The White House

The President's House, in L'Enfant's plan, balanced the Capitol at the far end of the great diagonal avenue linking the two buildings. At the same time, L'Enfant placed the Executive Mansion on a height that provided for an impressive prospect (to the south) to the point chosen for a monument to Washington and beyond down the Potomac River, which at that point turned south from its previous easterly direction. The misplacing of the Washington Monument off the planned southern axis is clearly seen in aerial views of the White House. The Sixteenth Street axis, on the other hand, runs true north from the more formal northern front of the White House as it faces on the residential facades surrounding Lafayette Square.

The White House setting changed in accordance with the varying tastes of its occupants. The north front during the administration of Abraham Lincoln was graced by a statue of Thomas Jefferson. During the administration of Benjamin Harrison, exotic plants dominated the north front. The south front has alternated from formal to rustic (sometimes with sheep grazing on the

lawn, as shown in figure 79; also see figure 3). As Thomas Jefferson was the originator of the classic style in American government buildings, so he was the originator of the informal parklike setting for the south grounds of the White House two decades before the English park style became popular in America.

FIGURE 80. *Letter from Thomas Jefferson to Thomas Munroe, 21 March 1803.*

Courtesy Library of Congress.

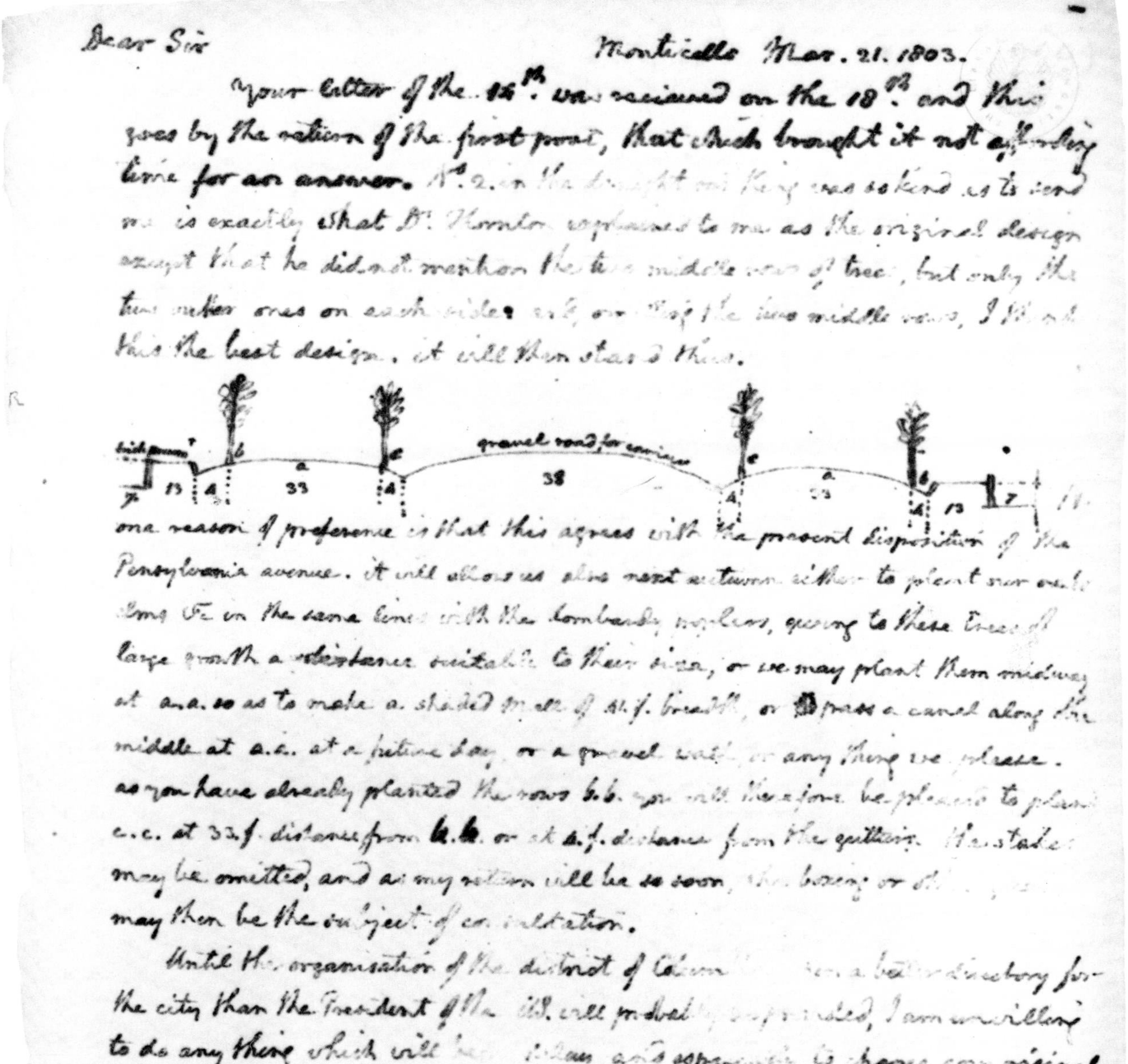

Dear Sir Monticello Mar. 21. 1803.

Your letter of the 16th. was recieved on the 18th. and this goes by the return of the first post, that which brought it not affording time for an answer. No. 2. in the draught you were so kind as to send me is exactly what Dr. Thornton explained to me as the original design except that he did not mention the two middle rows of trees, but only the two outer ones on each side. and omitting the two middle rows, I think this the best design. it will then stand thus.

gravel road for carriages
13 4 33 4 38 4 33 4 13 7
a b c

one reason of preference is that this agrees with the present disposition of the Pensylvania avenue. it will allow us also next autumn either to plant our oaks &c in the same lines with the Lombardy poplars, giving to these trees of large growth a distance suitable to their size, or we may plant them midway at a.a. so as to make a shaded mall of 51. f. breadth, or to pass a canal along the middle at a.a. at a future day, or a gravel walk or any thing we please. as you have already planted the rows b.b. you will therefore be pleased to plant c.c. at 33. f. distance from b.b. or at 4. f. distance from the gutters. the stakes may be omitted, and as my return will be so soon, the boxing or other guard may then be the subject of consultation.

Until the organisation of the district of Columbia gives a better directory for the city than the President of the US. will probably be provided, I am unwilling to do any thing which will bear delay, and especially to change any original destination of the public grounds. and as I shall be with you within one week after you recieve this, the report of the committee for the theatre shall be considered immediately on my return. be pleased to mention this to them and to accept my friendly salutations.

Th: Jefferson

Mr. Munroe

22510

FIGURE 81. *Pennsylvania Avenue, ca. 1870.*
This wood engraving was made by William
Roberts of New York.

Courtesy American Antiquarian Society,
Worcester, Massachusetts.

Pennsylvania Avenue

Pennsylvania Avenue is perhaps the most important street in the United States. It links the seat of legislative power, the Congress, with the seat of executive power, the president. Over the avenue pass the inaugural parades, when incoming presidents travel from the White House to the Capitol to take the oath of office. Thomas Jefferson was the first architect of the avenue, planting fast-growing Lombardy poplars and suggesting appropriate walkways and drainage ditches along its length (figure 80). Through much of the nineteenth century, however, the avenue remained a muddy and dusty thoroughfare. Late in the century, it was paved with wooden paving blocks (figure 81). An elegant design by Horace P. Russ to provide alternating black and white paving blocks for a central walkway down Pennsylvania Avenue was proposed in 1853 (figure 82).

142

Proposed plan for PAVING PENNSYLVANIA AVENUE Washington City D. C.

Designed by HORACE P. RUSS, New York.

"The Power To Stir Men's Minds"

"Make no little plans, for they have no power to stir men's minds." This injunction, attributed to Daniel Burnham, may serve as the motto for Washington's planning history.

People are rarely aware of the incremental growth of a city caused by the cumulative effect of thousands of individual planning decisions of private individuals or public officials. "Great plans" generate competing choices that must be made in any great city and thus they provide a stimulus to which citizens can react. Washington's planners have made no little plans, but big ones. L'Enfant, Downing, Burnham, Olmsted, McKim, Owings, the National Capital Planning Commission, the Commission of Fine Arts, the District government, and other individuals and agencies have strived to make the Nation's Capital worthy of its great past and hopeful future. Each plan has been modified to some degree by its successor, and the work is yet unfinished. For the process of creating a proud setting for the Nation's Capital continues still.

Bibliography For The Exhibition

The following books and articles can add immeasurably to the student's ability to perceive Washington in a visual and physical manner. The exhibition was designed to appeal in this fashion and to encourage the viewer to experience the city as a living exhibition in which each generation participates.

General Works

The most important single source for an understanding of how Washington "works" is Paul D. Spreiregen, ed., *On the Art of Designing Cities: Selected Essays of Elbert Peets* (Cambridge, Mass.: MIT Press, 1968). Less effective visually, but more detailed historically, is John W. Reps, *Monumental Washington: The Planning and Development of the Capital Center* (Princeton: Princeton University Press, 1967).

Specialized Studies of Washington Planning

A brilliant and incisive interpretation of L'Enfant's plan is J. P. Dougherty, "Baroque and Picturesque Motifs in L'Enfant's Design for the Federal Capital," *American Quarterly* 26, no. 1 (March 1974): 23–36. A sympathetic and revisionist account of Andrew Jackson Downing is Wilcomb E. Washburn, "Vision of Life for the Mall," *Journal of the American Institute of Architects* 47, no. 3 (March 1967): 52–59. William T. Partridge, "L'Enfant's Methods and Features of His Plan for the Federal City," a fine brief study, has been excerpted from the *Annual Report of the National Capital Park and Planning Commission, 1930,* and reprinted by the National Capital Planning Commission (Washington, D.C., 1975). A significant documentary collection is Saul K. Padover, ed., *Thomas Jefferson and the National Capital: Containing Notes and Correspondence exchanged between Jefferson, Washington, L'Enfant, Ellicott, Hallett, Thornton, Latrobe, the Commissioners, and others, relating to the founding, surveying, planning, designing, constructing, and administering of the City of Washington, 1783–1818* (Washington, D.C.: Government Printing Office, 1946). Charles Moore, *Problems in the Development of Washington* (offprint from the *Journal of the American Institute of Architects,* Washington, D.C., 1917), is the account by the key figure in the Senate Park Commission's work and later the chairman of the National Commission of Fine Arts. Moore, as clerk of the Senate Committee on the District of Columbia, had earlier edited *The Improvement of the Park System of the District of Columbia* (Washington, D.C.: Government Printing Office, 1902), which, along with Glenn Brown's compilation of *Papers Relating to the Improvement of the City of Washington, District of Columbia* (Washington, D.C.: Government Printing Office, 1901), and Moore's supplement, *Park Improvement Papers* (Washington, D.C.: Government Printing Office, 1902), provides the basis for understanding the work of the Senate Park Commission.

More recent planning initiatives in Washington are discussed in Paul Thiry, ed., *Washington in Transition* (Washington, D.C.: American Institute of Architects, 1963); reprint of *Journal of the American Institute of Architects* 39, no. 1 (January 1963), which included essays by architects, planners, and historians on the current state of planning in Washington. Paul D. Spreiregen's article, "The L'Enfant Plan for Washington," is a particularly notable contribution to the issue.

Studies of Special Locations in Washington   George J. Olszewski has written a number of short but thorough studies of special areas in the federal city. Published by various offices of the United States Department of the Interior, National Park Service, they have not had wide circulation. Among Olszewski's studies are *History of the Mall, Washington, D.C.* (March 1970); *The President's Park South, Washington, D.C.* (April 1970); *A History of the Washington Monument, 1844–1968* (April 1971); *Lincoln Park, Washington, D.C.* (July 1968); and *Lafayette Park* (1964). Other studies published by the National Park Service include Joan H. Stanley, *Judiciary Square, Washington, D.C.: A Park History* (July 1968); and Gordon Chapell, "Historic Resource Study: East and West Potomac Parks: A History" (June 1973; typescript issued by the Denver Service Center of the National Park Service). See also Cornelius W. Heine, *A History of National Capital Parks* (Washington, D.C.: Department of the Interior, 1953), which concentrates on the administrative history of National Capital Parks.

Pennsylvania Avenue, the grand axis linking the White House and the Capitol, has been the focal point of several specialized studies. Mary Cable, *The Avenue of the Presidents* (Boston: Houghton Mifflin Company, 1969), is light and popular but informed by the author's conversations with Nathaniel Owings, the architect of the Pennsylvania Avenue Redevelopment Plan, who has also supplied a foreword. *The Pennsylvania Avenue Plan 1974*, published by the Pennsylvania Avenue Development Corporation in October 1974 contains an extraordinarily thorough and perceptive study of the historical origins of planning for the avenue from L'Enfant's time to the present. *Pennsylvania Avenue: Report of the President's Council on Pennsylvania Avenue*, presented to the president in 1964, is an impressive account of the council's initial thoughts for the development of the avenue, enlivened by reproductions of the sketches of Nicholas Solovioff.

Specialized Studies of Buildings   Daniel D. Reiff, *Washington Architecture, 1791–1861: Problems in Development* (Washington, D.C.: U.S. Commission of Fine Arts, 1971), concentrates on architectural history, but considers also the over-all planning of L'Enfant and Downing. Diane Maddex, *Historic Buildings of Washington, D.C.* (Pitts-

146

burgh, Pa.: Ober Park Associates, 1973), a consideration in depth of a number of important Washington buildings, is based on the records of the Historic American Buildings Survey. A more comprehensive exposition of the HABS drawings of many Washington buildings is in *Historic American Buildings Survey: Catalog for the District of Columbia,* ed. Nancy Schwartz (Charlottesville, Va.: University Press of Virginia for the Columbia Historical Society, 1975). *Downtown Urban Renewal Area Landmarks, Washington, D.C.* (Washington, D.C., 1970), prepared by the National Capital Planning Commission in cooperation with the District of Columbia Redevelopment Land Agency, is an important study of the commission's role in landmark preservation.

Glenn Brown, *History of the United States Capitol,* 2 vols. (Washington, D.C.: Government Printing Office, 1901–1904; reprint ed., New York: Da Capo Press, 1970), is basic to the study of this most important of Washington's physical structures. Specialized studies of other Washington buildings include Mario E. Campioli, "The Original East Central Portico of the Capitol," *Capitol Studies* 1, no. 1 (Spring 1972): 73–85; Charles McLaughlin, "The Capitol in Peril? The West Front Controversy from Walter to Stewart," *Records of the Columbia Historical Society* 69–70 (1971): 237–65; John Y. Cole, "The Main Building of the Library of Congress, A Chronology, 1871–1965" (an album of photographs), and also "Smithmeyer & Pelz: Embattled Architects of the Library of Congress," *Quarterly Journal of the Library of Congress* 29, no. 4 (October 1972): 267–307; Wilcomb E. Washburn, "Temple of the Arts: The Renovation of Washington's Patent Office Building," *Journal of the American Institute of Architects* 51, no. 3 (March 1969): 54–61.

Donald Beekman Myer, *Bridges and the City of Washington* (Washington, D.C.: U.S. Commission of Fine Arts, 1974) is a fine study of Washington's bridges.

James M. Goode, *The Outdoor Sculpture of Washington, D.C.: A Comprehensive Historical Guide* (Washington, D.C.: Smithsonian Institution Press, 1974), is everything its subtitle promises. Goode is presently at work on a history of Washington's "lost" (i.e., destroyed) buildings.

Eleanor M. McPeck, "George Isham Parkyns: Artist and Landscape Architect, 1749-1820," *Quarterly Journal of the Library of Congress* 30, no. 3 (July 1973): 171–82, an important study of a little-known figure, contains significant information on the early layout of the White House grounds.

Cartographic Studies

Coolie Verner, "Surveying and Mapping the New Federal City: The First Printed Maps of Washington, D.C.," *Imago Mundi: A Review of Early Cartography* 23 (1969): 59–72, is a scholarly and technical account of the subject.

Herman R. Friis and Ralph E. Ehrenberg, "Nicholas King and His Wharfing Plans of the City of Washington, 1797," *Records of the Columbia Historical Society* 66–68 (1969): 34–46, is an important study based on King's plans in the National Archives. The article should be read in conjunction with Herman R. Friis, "Baron Alexander von Humboldt's Visit to Washington, D.C., June 1 through June 13, 1804," *Records of the Columbia Historical Society* 60–62 (1960–62): 1–35, as well as with Ralph E. Ehrenberg, "Nicholas King: First Surveyor of the City of Washington, 1803–1812," *Records of the Columbia Historical Society* 69–70 (1969–70): 31–65.

Catalogs of Exhibitions One of the earliest catalogs of materials relating to the planning of Washington is P. Lee Phillips, *The Beginnings of Washington as Described in Books, Maps, and Views* (Washington, D.C., 1917). A later catalog issued by the Library of Congress is *District of Columbia Sesquicentennial of the Establishment of the Permanent Seat of the Government: An Exhibition in the Library of Congress, Washington, D.C., April 24, 1950, to April 24, 1951* (Washington, D.C.: Government Printing Office, 1950).

Later the Library of Congress published *The Grand Design: An Exhibition Tracing the Evolution of the L'Enfant Plan and Subsequent Plans for the Development of Pennsylvania Avenue and the Mall Area, Organized Jointly by the Library of Congress and the President's Temporary Commission on Pennsylvania Avenue* (Washington, D.C., 1967).

The National Archives published *Washington—The Design of the Federal City* in 1972. The catalog portrays some of the Archives' rich collections relating to the history of Washington planning. The National Collection of Fine Arts of the Smithsonian Institution published a catalog, entitled *Art for Architecture: Washington, D.C. 1895–1925,* in conjunction with an exhibition in 1975.

Walking Tours No entirely successful walking tour guide of Washington exists though the two best are probably *Washington, D.C.: Walking Tours,* written by Tony P. Wrenn, edited and produced by the Preservation Press, National Trust for Historic Preservation (Washington, D.C., 1975), and *A Guide to the Architecture of Washington, D.C.,* compiled by the editorial board of the Washington Metropolitan Chapter of the American Institute of Architects under the chairmanship of Hugh Newell Jacobsen (Washington, D.C., 1965; 2d edn., 1974).

CATALOG

OF THE EXHIBITION

THE FEDERAL CITY

Because many exhibition items are requested on loan, this list is subject to revision. A fully annotated copy of the items exhibited is on deposit at the Smithsonian Institution Libraries.

LOCATING WASHINGTON

Bandanna Map of the City of Washington, D.C.; copy of first map of Washington, 1792, engraved by Samuel Hill; linen; Political History Division of the Museum of History and Technology, Smithsonian Institution; reproduced in this book as the frontispiece.

Students Studying the Layout of the City; Scene in a Public School Classroom in Washington, ca. 1900; photograph by Frances Benjamin Johnston; courtesy Library of Congress Prints and Photographs Division; reproduced in this book as figure 15.

A Map of the Country between Albemarle Sound and Lake Erie, ca. 1787; map; courtesy Library of Congress Map Division.

Topographical Map of the Ten-Mile Square Area That Includes the City of Washington as Designed by Pierre L'Enfant, 1793; map; drawn by Andrew Ellicott; courtesy Library of Congress Map Division; reproduced in this book as figure 2.

Great Falls; photograph by Robert C. Lautman.

George Town and Federal City, or City of Washington, 1801; aquatint engraving colored by hand; drawn by A. Beck of Philadelphia; engraved by T. Cartwright of London; courtesy Columbia Historical Society.

Panoramic View of Washington City from the New Dome of the Capitol, Looking West, 1852; lithograph; drawn from nature and printed by Edward Sachse; courtesy Columbia Historical Society.

Panoramic View of Washington from the Potomac, 1862; lithograph colored by hand, by L. N. Rosenthal; courtesy Columbia Historical Society; reproduced as the cover illustration for this book.

Bird's-Eye View of the City of Washington, D.C., and the Seat of War in Virginia; lithograph; published by John Bachmann; courtesy Columbia Historical Society.

Elements of National Thrift and Empire; lithograph; design by J. G. Bruff; lithography by E. Weber & Company, Baltimore, Maryland; courtesy Columbia Historical Society.

Aerial View of Washington, D.C.; photograph by Perkin-Elmer; Smithsonian Institution.

PLANNING WASHINGTON

View of Washington, Looking East, from Arlington National Cemetery, 1975; tomb of Pierre Charles L'Enfant in foreground; photograph by Staples & Charles; reproduced in this book as figure 30.

Thomas Jefferson's Plan for the City of Washington; drawing dated March 1791; photograph; courtesy Library of Congress Manuscript Division; reproduced in this book as figure 31.

Pierre L'Enfant's Letter of Application; dated 11 September 1789; photographic reproduction; courtesy Library of Congress Manuscript Division.

L'Enfant's Plan; photographic enlargement; National Capital Planning Commission.

Streets Radiating from the White House; photographs by Robert C. Lautman.

Andrew Ellicott Map; photographic enlargement; National Capital Planning Commission.

Andrew Ellicott; ivory miniature painted with oils; Museum of History and Technology, Smithsonian Institution; reproduced in this book as figure 32.

[Benjamin Banneker] *Bannaker's* [sic] *Maryland, Pennsylvania, Delaware, Virginia, Kentucky and North Carolina Almanack and Ephemeris For the Year of our Lord 1796; Being Bissextile, or Leap-Year: The Twentieth Year of the American independence and Eighth Year of the Federal Government;* book; courtesy Maryland Historical Society.

PIERRE L'ENFANT

Andrew Jackson Downing; photograph of a daguerreotype; courtesy George B. Tatum; reproduced in this book as figure 33.

Downing Plan; photograph; courtesy National Archives.

Downing's Proposals for a Suspension Bridge across the Canal (now Constitution Avenue) and for a President's Arch at the End of Pennsylvania Avenue; excerpt from Downing's 1851 "Explanatory Notes"; courtesy National Archives; reproduced in this book as figure 34.

Andrew Jackson Downing to Joseph Henry; letter; dated 14 June 1851; Smithsonian Institution Archives.

Aerial View of the Mall in the Vicinity of the Smithsonian Institution, ca. 1930; photograph by U.S. Army Air Corps; courtesy Commission of Fine Arts; reproduced in this book as figure 36.

Trees on the Mall; a group of contemporary photographs by Staples & Charles.

"Washington, D.C.," showing projected improvements; lithograph, ca. 1852; published by Smith & Jenkins, New York; courtesy Columbia Historical Society; reproduced in this book on p. 166.

Sketch of the U.S. Capitol, 1858; watercolor by Joacim Ferdinand Richardt; Political History Division of the Museum of History and Technology, Smithsonian Institution; reproduced in this book as figure 35.

ANDREW JACKSON DOWNING

Map of the District of Columbia, 1857; prepared by A. Boschke; map; courtesy Library of Congress Map Division.

Hints on Public Architecture, by Robert Dale Owen (New York and London: George P. Putnam, 1849); book; Smithsonian Institution Libraries.

Exhibition of Natural History Specimens, 1865; Great Hall, Smithsonian Institution Building; photograph; Smithsonian Institution Archives.

Buffalo on the Smithsonian Grounds; photograph; Smithsonian Institution Archives.

Secretary Joseph Henry's Office; East Wing, Smithsonian Institution Building, ca. 1862; photograph; Smithsonian Institution Archives.

First Floor of the South Tower Used as Children's Museum; Smithsonian Institution Building, ca. 1902; photograph; Smithsonian Institution Archives.

The Smithsonian Institution Building and the Capitol in the 1860s; photograph by Mathew Brady; courtesy National Archives Audiovisual Division; reproduced in this book as figure 37.

Smithsonian Park, 1882; colored drawing by J. Stewart; courtesy National Archives Cartographic Archives Division.

Model of Smithsonian Building, 1847; constructed by the architect, James Renwick, Jr.; wood and paper, painted; Smithsonian Institution.

JAMES McMILLAN AND THE SENATE PARK COMMISSION
Senator James McMillan; photograph; Commission of Fine Arts.

Daniel Hudson Burnham; photograph; courtesy Library of Congress Prints and Photographs Division; reproduced in this book as figure 38.

Charles F. McKim; photograph by Frances Benjamin Johnston; courtesy Library of Congress Prints and Photographs Division.

Frederick Law Olmsted, Jr.; photograph; Commission of Fine Arts.

Augustus Saint-Gaudens; photograph by George Cox; Photographic History Division of the Museum of History and Technology, Smithsonian Institution.

C. A. Spring-Rice to Charles McKim; letter; courtesy New York Public Library, Charles McKim Papers, Manuscripts and Archives Division, Astor, Lenox, and Tilden Foundations.

Proposed Design of Senate Park Commission for Grouping of Memorial Buildings, 1902; photograph; Commission of Fine Arts.

Proposed Design of Senate Park Commission for Grouping of Executive Buildings on Lafayette Square; photograph; courtesy National Archives.

Map of the District of Columbia Showing Areas Recommended To Be Taken as Necessary for New Parks and Park Connections; compiled and drawn in the office of the Commission on the Improvement of the Park System; November 1901; photolithograph by A. Hoen and Company, Baltimore, Maryland; courtesy Library of Congress Map Division.

Aerial View of the Mall; view looking west from the Capitol; photograph; Commission of Fine Arts.

Aerial View of the Mall; looking east and showing planting of elms in 1930s; photograph; Commission of Fine Arts; reproduced in this book as figure 42.

Cartoon by Jim Berryman; published in the *Washington Evening Star*, 14 January 1908; photograph; courtesy *Washington Star* and Library of Congress Newspaper Division; reproduced in this book as figure 43.

The Mall, 1975; a group of photographs by Staples & Charles.

Three-dimensional Model of the City of Washington as It Existed in 1901; photograph; Commission of Fine Arts; reproduced in this book as figure 39.

Three-dimensional Model of the Design Proposed by the Senate Park Commission for the Mall and Capitol Grounds, 1901–1902; photograph; Commission of Fine Arts; reproduced in this book as figure 44.

Model Makers Working on Senate Park Commission Models; created for an exhibition at the Corcoran Gallery, Washington, D.C., February 1902; photograph; Commission of Fine Arts.

The Tuileries Gardens; view along the major axis from the Arc du Carrousel to the Arc de Triomphe, showing the obelisk marking the cross axis at the Place de la Concorde, Paris; photographic enlargement made by the Senate Park Commission for their exhibition of 1902; Commission of Fine Arts; reproduced in this book as figure 40.

The Arc de Triomphe; view along the axis of the Champs Élysées, Paris; photographic enlargement; Commission of Fine Arts.

Members of Senate Park Commission during European Tour, 1901; photograph; Commission of Fine Arts.

View of Long Walk at Windsor, near London; photographic enlargement; Commission of Fine Arts; reproduced in this book as figure 41.

Fontana di Acqua Marcia Piazza di Termini, Rome; photographic enlargement; Commission of Fine Arts.

Washington Plan for 1901; watercolor rendering drawn in 1902 by F. L. V. Hoppin; Commission of Fine Arts.

Detail of Senate Park Commission Plan of 1901–1902; Washington Monument and Monument Gardens; watercolor rendering drawn in 1902 by C. Graham; Commission of Fine Arts.

REJECTED PLANS

Nicholas King Wharfing Plans of the City of Washington, 1797, Sheet 3; colored drawing by Nicholas King; courtesy National Archives Cartographic Archives Division.

Nicholas King Wharfing Plans of the City of Washington, 1797, Sheet 9; photographic reproduction of colored drawing by Nicholas King; courtesy National Archives Cartographic Archives Division.

"Plan of the West end of the public Appropriation in the city of Washington, called the Mall, as proposed to be arranged for the Site of the University. To the Committee of the House of Representatives of Congress"; dated 4 January 1816; manuscript plan by Benjamin Latrobe; courtesy Library of Congress Map Division; reproduced in this book as figure 45.

"Plan of the Mall with the adjoining Streets and Avenues; the relative position of the Capitol, President's House, and other Public Buildings; and particularly the improvement of that part of the Mall, situated between Seventh and Twelfth Streets; with a view to a Botanic Garden, connected with the establishment of the Smithsonian Institution, proposed to be in charge of the National Institution for the promotion of Science"; dated 16 February 1841; colored drawing by Robert Mills; courtesy National Archives Cartographic Archives Division.

"Scheme for location of Memorial Bridge and Monuments: Grouping of Public Buildings and Improvement of the Mall, Washington, D.C."; dated 10 October 1901; watercolor by George Keller; courtesy American Antiquarian Society; reproduced in this book as figure 46.

LOST WASHINGTON *Prisoners to a Grid,* 1973; charcoal on paper, mylar, and metalized mylar; drawing by Nancy Wolf; courtesy Mr. and Mrs. Stan Steppa; reproduced in this book as figure 47.

Convention Hall Market (Northern Liberty Market), Fifth and K Streets, NW, 1928; photograph; courtesy *Washington Star* and National Geographic Society; reproduced in this book as figure 48.

Northern Liberty Market building, 1976; photograph by Robert C. Lautman.

Corcoran House, Connecticut Avenue and H Street, NW, 1821–1921; photograph; courtesy National Park Service, U.S. Department of Interior; reproduced in this book as figure 49.

Interior of Corcoran House; photograph by Frances Benjamin Johnston; courtesy Library of Congress Prints and Photographs Division.

All Souls Unitarian Church, Sixth and D Streets, NW, 1822–1906; photograph; courtesy Columbia Historical Society.

Church of the Covenant; photograph; courtesy J. Alexander.

Douglas Row, Eye Street between Second and Third Streets, NW; photograph; courtesy Columbia Historical Society.

Old Capitol Building, First and A Streets, NE; view after building had been converted into Trumbull's Row; photograph by Leets Brothers of Washington; courtesy George Washington University Wright Collection.

Old Capitol Building; erected in 1815 as temporary seat of U.S. Congress and later used as a prison; photograph by Mathew Brady; courtesy Library of Congress Prints and Photographs Division.

Carroll Row, First Street, SE, between East Capitol Street and Pennsylvania Avenue, ca. 1885; photograph by L. C. Handy; courtesy National Geographic Society.

Carberry House, Seventeenth and C Streets, NW; photograph; courtesy Columbia Historical Society.

U.S. Soldiers' Home Library; photograph; courtesy Martin Luther King Memorial Library (D.C. Public Library).

Interior of Gelman's Drug Store, 627 Pennsylvania Avenue, NW, 1967; photographed by George Eisenman; courtesy Historic American Buildings Survey.

Army Medical Museum Building, Seventh Street and Independence Avenue, SW, 1969; photograph by Ronald Comedy; courtesy Historic American Buildings Survey.

Esso Building at Constitution Avenue and Second Street, NW, 1932–69; photograph; Commission of Fine Arts.

Shepherd's Row, Connecticut Avenue and K Street, NW; photograph; courtesy Columbia Historical Society.

Townhouse façade, 1905 F Street, NW, 1969; photograph by Ronald Comedy; courtesy Historic American Buildings Survey.

Townhouse façade, 1911 F Street, NW, 1969; photograph by Ronald Comedy; courtesy Historic American Buildings Survey.

CURRENT PLANS

Comprehensive Plan for the National Capital and Its Environs, adopted Pursuant to the National Capital Planning Act of 1952, as amended; book; National Capital Planning Commission.

Housing Plan for Eighth Street Axis; colored drawing; courtesy Pennsylvania Avenue Development Corporation.

Four Perspective Models; Mall area as it might have looked had the plans of L'Enfant, Downing, and the McMillan Commission been carried fully into execution and if present Comprehensive Plan is carried into execution; models constructed by Staples & Charles.

Memorandum for the Heads of Executive Departments and Establishments and the Commissioners of the District of Columbia; signed by President John F. Kennedy; dated 27 November 1962; reproduction of typescript; National Capital Planning Commission.

Sketch of Proposed New National Square, 1964; ink drawing by Nicholas Solovioff; courtesy Pennsylvania Avenue Development Corporation.

Sketch of Proposed Pershing Square, 1975; colored drawing; courtesy Pennsylvania Avenue Development Corporation.

The Radial Corridor Plan; reproduction of drawing; National Capital Planning Commission.

SECTIONAL DIVISIONS AND RIVALRIES IN THE DISTRICT OF COLUMBIA

Facts and Figures Showing the Discrimination Against the Eastern Portion of the District in Relation to Street Improvements, & c. (Washington, D.C.: R. O. Polkinhorn, Printer, 1883); booklet; courtesy Columbia Historical Society.

Map of Washington, 1976; National Capital Planning Commission.

WHO'S IN CHARGE HERE? *The Urban Planners, 1973;* pencil on paper; drawing by Nancy Wolf; courtesy Miss Frances.

Pen and ink drawing by Saul Steinberg; number 33 in the 1973 Smithsonian exhibition, "Steinberg at the Smithsonian, The Metamorphoses of an Emblem"; courtesy Karen Johnson Keland.

Proposed Urban Design Concepts; prepared by the National Capital Planning Commission, 1972; map; National Capital Planning Commission.

MODELS Restored Central Section of Model of the Design Proposed by the Senate Park Commission for the Mall and Capitol Grounds, 1901–1902; Commission of Fine Arts.

Restored Central Section of Model of the City of Washington as It Existed in 1901; Commission of Fine Arts.

Model; showing current plan for central monumental area; Pennsylvania Avenue Development Corporation.

Model; showing proposed Eighth Street multi-use building to include offices, shops, housing, and archives record storage; Pennsylvania Avenue Development Corporation.

ELEMENTS OF PLANNING

"Palisades of the Potomac," 1890; colored lithograph; copyright by Jacob Clark and E. B. Cottrell; courtesy American Antiquarian Society; reproduced in this book as figure 51.

Breuninger-Built Homes in the National Capital (Washington, D.C.: L. E. Breuninger & Sons, Builders-Realtors, 1925); book; Wilcomb E. Washburn.

800–820 Twenty-first Street, NE; photograph; courtesy National Archives Audiovisual Division.

Aerial View of Rockville, Maryland, by Fairchild Aerial Services, Inc.; reproduced in this book as figure 24.

Montgomery Village near Gaithersburg, Maryland; photograph by Staples & Charles.

"Le Droit Park Illustrated," Part I (Washington, D.C.: R. Beresford, Printer, 1877; published in the interest of A. L. Barber & Company, proprietors of Le Droit Park); courtesy Columbia Historical Society.

Purdy's Court, a Back Alley near the Capitol Grounds, Washington, D.C., 1908; photograph by Lewis Wickes Hine; courtesy International Museum of Photography at George Eastman House; reproduced in this book as figure 52.

Temple Court, SW, entrance between First and Canal Streets; photograph; courtesy Martin Luther King Memorial Library (D.C. Public Library).

Maps of the District of Columbia and City of Washington (Washington, D.C.: A. Boyd Hamilton, 1852); book; courtesy Columbia Historical Society.

Views of Restored Alleys in Washington, D.C.; photographs by Staples & Charles.

The Federal Triangle, ca. 1940; photograph by Fairchild Aerial Services, Inc.; courtesy Commission of Fine Arts; reproduced in this book as figure 53.

The State, War and Navy Building, 1871–88; photograph by C. S. Cudlip & Company; courtesy Boston Public Library; reproduced in this book as figure 54.

The Pentagon; color photograph; courtesy U.S. Navy Information Center.

Interior of the Pension Building; photograph; courtesy Historic American Buildings Survey.

Interior View of the Pension Building; stereo card; courtesy Staples & Charles.

Patent Office Building (now the National Collection of Fine Arts and National Portrait Gallery); photographic reproduction of daguerreotype attributed to John Plumbe, Jr., 1846; courtesy Library of Congress Prints and Photographs Division.

Interior View of Third Floor of Patent Office Building (National Portrait Gallery) after Restoration, 1975; photograph; National Portrait Gallery, Smithsonian Institution.

City Post Office; photograph; courtesy National Archives Audiovisual Division.

SUBURBS

ALLEYS

PUBLIC BUILDINGS AND FEDERAL OFFICES

Proposed Design for Remodeling the State, War and Navy Building (Executive Office Building); photograph; Commission of Fine Arts.

DISTRICT SCHOOLS AND LIBRARIES Franklin School, ca. 1900; photograph by Frances Benjamin Johnston; courtesy Library of Congress Prints and Photographs Division; reproduced in this book as figure 56.

New Schools in Washington, D.C., 1975; a group of photographs by Staples & Charles.

Martin Luther King Memorial Library; photograph; courtesy Martin Luther King Memorial Library (D.C. Public Library).

DISTRICT MARKETS Center Market; photograph; courtesy Columbia Historical Society.

Farmers' Stands at Center Market, 1927; photograph; courtesy National Archives Audiovisual Division.

Scene at Eastern Market, ca. 1890; photograph; courtesy Martin Luther King Memorial Library (D.C. Public Library); reproduced in this book as figure 55.

Scenes at Eastern Market, 1975; photographs by Staples & Charles.

EDUCATIONAL INSTITUTIONS Preliminary Plan for Laying Out Buildings and Grounds of the American University, Washington, D.C.; dated 19 January 1895; designed by Olmsted, Olmsted, & Eliot; printed plan; courtesy Charles McLaughlin.

The Army War College (now the National War College) and Washington Channel; photograph by U.S. Army Air Corps; courtesy Commission of Fine Arts; reproduced in this book as figure 58.

Plan of Layout of Buildings and Grounds for the War College and Engineer Post; photograph; courtesy National War College.

The Columbia Institution for the Deaf and Dumb (Gallaudet College), 1885; isometrical view drawn by Glenn Brown, Jr.; photolithograph by N. Peters; courtesy Gallaudet College; reproduced in this book as figure 57.

Views of Gallaudet College, 1975; photographs by Robert C. Lautman.

BRIDGES Pennsylvania Avenue Bridge over Rock Creek Park, ca. 1862; photograph by A. J. Russell; courtesy Library of Congress Prints and Photographs Division.

Cabin John Bridge, with Capital Bicycle Club in Foreground; dated 13 May 1883; photograph; courtesy Columbia Historical Society.

William Howard Taft Bridge over Rock Creek Park; photograph; courtesy Library of Congress Prints and Photographs Division.

Illustration from *Prospective Designs and Estimates for the Memorial Bridge Across the Potomac River*, prepared by the J. Deering Reed Company, to Members of the Fifty-seventh Congress (Boston: J. C. Clark & Co., Printers, 1901); photograph; courtesy Library of Congress.

Memorial Bridge, 1931; photograph; courtesy National Archives Audiovisual Division.

Memorial Bridge; President Kennedy's Funeral Procession, 26 November 1963; photograph; courtesy *Washington Post.*

Proposed Washington Channel Bridge; elevation; photographic reduction by Staples & Charles.

Cross Section of Proposed Washington Channel Bridge; sketch by Chloethiel Woodard Smith; courtesy of the architect; reproduced in this book as figure 60.

Washington Channel Bridge Model; photograph from report, "A Washington Channel Bridge," 1966; prepared by Chloethiel Woodard Smith and Associates; courtesy National Capital Parks, U.S. Department of Interior.

Theodore Roosevelt Bridge, 1975; photograph by Robert C. Lautman; reproduced in this book as figure 59.

Memorial Bridge; photograph by Robert C. Lautman.

CIRCLES

Aerial view of Logan Circle, 1950; photograph by Elwood Baker; courtesy *Washington Star;* reproduced in this book as figure 61.

Composite Drawing and Photograph of Logan Circle Area, 1975; photograph; courtesy Turner Associates.

Drawings of Townhouse Façades, Logan Circle area; photograph; courtesy Turner Associates.

Logan Circle, 1975; photograph by Robert C. Lautman.

Aerial view of Dupont Circle; photograph by Fairchild Aerial Surveys, Inc.; courtesy Commission of Fine Arts.

WATER

The Canal and the Capitol, July 1861; photograph; courtesy Library of Congress Prints and Photographs Division.

Traffic on the C & O Canal, ca. 1910; photograph; courtesy Columbia Historical Society Proctor Collection; reproduced in this book as figure 62.

Potomac at Mouth of Canal, September 25, 1850; watercolor by Montgomery Meigs; Political History Division of the Museum of History and Technology, Smithsonian Institution.

Canoes on the C & O Canal, 1962; photograph; courtesy National Capital Parks, U.S. Department of Interior.

Washington from Single Tree Hill, 1856; watercolor by John Savile Lumly; courtesy Columbia Historical Society.

View from East Potomac Park across Washington Channel; photograph; courtesy National Capital Parks, U.S. Department of Interior.

TREES

Tree-lined K Street, NW, ca. 1915; photograph; courtesy National Geographic Society; reproduced in this book as figure 63.

Virginia Avenue, SW; photograph; Commission of Fine Arts.

The West Front of the U.S. Capitol, with the Ulysses S. Grant Memorial and Reflecting Pool; photograph by Robert C. Lautman; courtesy of the photographer; reproduced in this book as figure 75.

Tree-lined Street; photograph; courtesy National Geographic Society.

New Hampshire Avenue at Eighteenth Street, NW, ca. 1900; photograph; Commission of Fine Arts.

Virginia Avenue, SW, 1975; photograph by Staples & Charles.

Streets, Washington, D.C., 1975; photographs by Staples & Charles.

VISTAS Vista of the Capitol from the Soldiers' Home Grounds, early 1900s; photograph; Political History Division of the Museum of History and Technology, Smithsonian Institution; reproduced in this book as figure 64.

Hypothetical View of the Smithsonian Institution Building from Tenth Street, SW; drawing by Robert Staples; reproduced in this book as figure 65.

Aerial view of the White House Grounds and Sixteenth Street, NW; photograph by Fairchild Aerial Surveys, Inc.; courtesy Commission of Fine Arts.

A Series of Vistas in Washington, D.C., 1975; Pennsylvania and New York Avenues, Tenth and Eighth Streets, NW, included; photographs by Robert C. Lautman.

AIRPORTS Dulles International Airport at Night; designed by Eero Saarinen; photograph; Federal Aviation Agency, U.S. Department of Transportation; reproduced in this book as figure 66.

Mobile Lounges at Dulles International Airport; photograph by Staples & Charles.

Aerial View of Dulles International Airport; photograph by National Ocean Survey; courtesy U.S. Department of Commerce.

View of Washington, D.C., from National Airport; photograph by Robert C. Lautman.

Aerial View of National Airport; photograph; Commission of Fine Arts.

RAILROADS Aerial View of Union Station; photograph; courtesy National Archives Audiovisual Division.

Union Station Lobby, ca. 1908; photograph; courtesy Library of Congress Prints and Photographs Division; reproduced in this book as figure 67.

Baltimore & Ohio Railroad Station; photograph; courtesy Martin Luther King Memorial Library (D.C. Public Library).

View of Pennsylvania Railroad Station on the Mall in a Snowstorm, ca. 1900; photograph; Commission of Fine Arts.

View of Railroad Tracks Leading into Union Station; photograph; courtesy Library of Congress Prints and Photographs Division.

METRO Metro Station and New Subway Cars, June 1975; photograph; courtesy Washington Metropolitan Area Transit Authority; reproduced in this book as figure 68.

Washington Metropolitan Area Metro Map; courtesy Washington Metropolitan Area Transit Authority.

Tunnel under Construction, March 1974; photograph by Paul Myatt; courtesy Washington Metropolitan Area Transit Authority.

Metro Center Station, September 1975; photograph by Paul Myatt; courtesy Washington Metropolitan Area Transit Authority.

PARKWAYS AND HIGHWAYS

View of Washington, D.C., from the George Washington Memorial Parkway, Looking South; photograph by Robert C. Lautman.

Parking Lots in Washington, D.C.; photographs by Staples & Charles.

A Parking Lot in the Federal Triangle; photograph by Robert C. Lautman.

Rush-Hour Traffic on Pennsylvania Avenue; photograph by Robert C. Lautman.

View of New York Avenue, Looking South; photograph by Staples & Charles.

Views of the George Washington Memorial Parkway; photographs by David R. Allison, Staples & Charles.

Morning Rush-Hour Traffic on the Southeast/Southwest Freeway, 13 July 1975; view looking toward the Washington Monument; photograph by Ken Feil; courtesy *Washington Post*; reproduced in this book as figure 69.

Aerial View of Foggy Bottom Loop Interchange, Looking North, 1965; photograph; courtesy *Washington Post*.

Aerial View of Key Bridge, Whitehurst Freeway, and M Street, NW; photograph; courtesy National Geographic Society.

PARKS

Winter Scene, East Potomac Park; photograph; courtesy National Capital Parks, U.S. Department of Interior.

Lafayette Park in Winter; photograph; courtesy *Washington Post*.

Cascade and Reflecting Pool; view looking north from the sundial, Meridian Hill Park (now Malcolm X Park); photograph by John Ferrell; courtesy Library of Congress Prints and Photographs Division.

East Potomac Park, ca. 1925; photograph; Commission of Fine Arts; reproduced in this book as figure 70.

Sailboat Races, Lincoln Memorial Reflecting Pool, July 1928; photograph by Charles Martin; courtesy National Geographic Society.

View of the Lincoln Memorial, Smithsonian Institution Festival of American Folklife, and the Plantings of Constitution Gardens; photograph by David R. Allison, Staples & Charles; reproduced in this book as figure 74.

Vista in Rock Creek Park; photograph; courtesy Library of Congress Prints and Photographs Division.

Horseback Riding, Rock Creek Park; photograph; courtesy National Capital Parks, U.S. Department of Interior.

Winter Scene, Rock Creek Park; photograph; courtesy National Capital Parks, U.S. Department of Interior.

Iceskating, Rock Creek Park; photograph; Smithsonian Institution Archives; reproduced in this book as figure 70a.

Pierce Mill, Rock Creek Park; photograph by Staples & Charles.

Activities in the Parks, Washington, D.C.; a group of photographs by Staples & Charles.

THE MONUMENTAL CORE

Design for Completing the Washington Monument, 31 May 1877; pencil and ink sketch by Montgomery C. Meigs; courtesy National Archives Cartographic Archives Division.

Sketch of the Washington National Monument; watercolor by Robert Mills; courtesy National Archives Cartographic Archives Division; reproduced in this book as figure 77.

Design for Completion of the Washington Monument, proposed by Lewis Trezevant Cruger, Charleston, S.C.; newsclip; courtesy National Archives Cartographic Archives Division.

"Plan for Completing the Great Washington Monument, Correctly," 1876; ink drawing by J. Goldsborough Bruff; courtesy National Archives Cartographic Archives Division.

Plan for a Washington Monument; drawing by George Bridport; courtesy Library Company of Philadelphia.

"The Unfinished Monument of George Washington"; animated film by Benjamin Lawless; courtesy Benjamin Lawless.

Scissors Obelisk Monument (Scissors Closed); poster by Claes Oldenburg for the National Collection of Fine Arts, 1968; courtesy Library of Congress Prints and Photographs Division.

Washington Monument, 1975; photograph by Staples & Charles.

THE WHITE HOUSE The South Portico of the White House; photograph; courtesy Library of Congress Prints and Photographs Division.

"President's Mansion, North View," 1891; photograph; courtesy Library of Congress Prints and Photographs Division.

The White House during Lincoln's Administration; view of the statue of Thomas Jefferson, in foreground; photograph; courtesy Library of Congress Prints and Photographs Division.

"The President's House from the River"; steel line engraving; colored by hand; from Bartlett and Willis's *American Scenery* (London, 1840); courtesy Columbia Historical Society.

Aerial View of the White House Grounds, Ellipse, and the Washington Monument; photograph by Todd Aerial Mapping Service; courtesy National Capital Planning Commission.

Aerial View of the Ellipse, ca. 1905; photograph; courtesy National Archives Audiovisual Division.

"The White House," 1916; pencil on paper drawing by Childe Hassam; courtesy The White House Collection.

Letter from Thomas Jefferson to Thomas Munroe; dated 21 March 1803; **PENNSYLVANIA AVENUE**
photograph; courtesy Library of Congress Manuscript Division; reproduced
in this book as figure 80.

"View of Capitol, Washington, D.C.," 1824; watercolor by Burton Charles;
photograph; courtesy Metropolitan Museum of Art, Purchase 1942, Joseph
Pulitzer Bequest.

View of the Capitol; sepia watercolor drawing by W. H. Bartlett; courtesy
Columbia Historical Society.

Proposed Plan for Paving Pennsylvania Avenue, Washington, D.C., 1853;
lithograph; designed by Horace P. Russ, New York; courtesy Columbia Historical Society; reproduced in this book as figure 82.

Pennsylvania Avenue, 1861; view looking east; photograph; courtesy Martin
Luther King Memorial Library (D.C. Public Library).

Pennsylvania Avenue, Washington, D.C.; wood engraving by William Roberts; courtesy American Antiquarian Society; reproduced in this book as
figure 81.

Nineteenth-Century Wood Paving Blocks from Division of Transportation;
gift of Thomas N. Scrotch; courtesy Smithsonian Institution.

Pennsylvania Avenue from the Treasury Building, 1875; line engraving;
colored by hand; courtesy Columbia Historical Society.

View of Pennsylvania Avenue from the Treasury Building, ca. 1892; photograph; courtesy Martin Luther King Memorial Library (D.C. Public Library).

View of Pennsylvania Avenue from the Treasury Building Looking towards
the Capitol, 1895; watercolor by Walter Paris; courtesy The White House
Collection.

Pennsylvania Avenue from the Treasury, 1900; photograph; courtesy Martin
Luther King Memorial Library (D.C. Public Library).

View of the White House and Pennsylvania Avenue from the State, War and
Navy Building (Executive Office Building), 1904; stereo card; courtesy Staples
& Charles.

Theodore Roosevelt's Inauguration Parade, Pennsylvania Avenue, 1905; photograph; courtesy Martin Luther King Memorial Library (D.C. Public Library).

Traffic on Pennsylvania Avenue; photograph; courtesy Columbia Historical
Society.

Proposed Traffic Viaduct for Pennsylvania Avenue, 1925; photograph; courtesy *Washington Post.*

View of Pennsylvania Avenue from Treasury, 1975; photograph by Staples &
Charles.

1	Navy Department	
2	War do.	
3	President's House	
4	Treasury & State Dep.ts	
5	Willard's Hotel	
6	Irving Hotel	
7	Patent Office	
8	Post do	
9	City Hall	
10	Brown's Hotel	

WASHINGTON, D.C.

Published by Smith & Jenkins, Lithographers and Engravers.

Ocean Bank Building 218 Fulton St.

NEW YORK

11	National Hotel
12	R.R. Depot
13	Capitol
14	Smithsonian Inst.
15	National Theatre
16	Suspension Bridge
17	Entrance to Public Grounds
18	Canal
19	Public Grounds, designed by A.J. Downing.

INDEX